VIRGINIA CITY

To Dance with the Devil

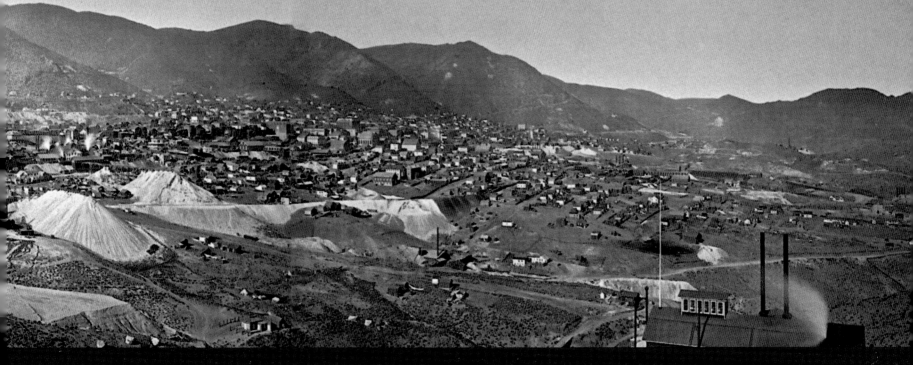

Nicholas Clapp

SUNBELT PUBLICATIONS
San Diego

Virginia City: To Dance with the Devil

Sunbelt Publications, Inc.
Copyright © 2016 by Nicholas Clapp
All rights reserved. First edition 2016

Cover and book design by Lydia D'moch
Edited by Anita Palmer
Project management by Deborah Young
Printed in Korea

Sunbelt Publications, Inc.
P.O. Box 191126
San Diego, CA 92159-1126
(619) 258-4911, fax (619) 258-4916
www.sunbeltbooks.com

20 19 18 17 16   5 4 3 2 1

Library of Congress Cataloging-in-Publication Data
Clapp, Nicholas.
Virginia City: To dance with the devil/by Nicholas Clapp.—First edition.
pages cm
Includes index.
ISBN 978-1-941384-15-2 (softcover : alk. paper)
1. Virginia City (Nev.)—History—19th century. I. Title.
F849.V8C58 2016
979.3'56—dc23
2015013698

Cover:
An1875 bird's-eye view; Adolph Sutro, a Virginia City force to be reckoned with.

Pages ii–iii
In 1876, the year after Virginia City was nearly leveled in a disastrous fire,
Carleton E. Watkins documented its amazing rebuilding and recovery with
a specially constructed "Mammoth" camera; it exposed three 16" x 20" glass
plates that together created a five-foot panorama.

Pages vi–vii:
Would-be tough customers in a Virginia City thirst parlor.
There were well over a hundred such saloons.

Dedicated to the memory of a rowdy good friend, Billy Varga.
With his wife, Melody, at his side, he was a last Virginia City "honest miner."

The story goes that Billy was buried in a cave-in—that is, all but his nose.
Frantically dug from the rubble, he was rushed to a Carson City hospital,
where doctors patched him as best they could.

The next morning, his hospital bed was empty.

To hell with the hurt, he was back in his mine, drilling and blasting.
Assays of silver in a vein he'd been working were promising.
It could widen; it could yield a half-million dollars!

Billy lived hard, was ever hopeful, and died young.
He rests in a byway of Virginia City's Silver Terrace cemeteries.

CONTENTS

The bustling *Territorial Enterprise*.

AUTHOR'S NOTES

Considering that a prime source for much of what's known of Virginia City—the *Territorial Enterprise*—"never hesitated about devising when the public needed matters of thrilling interest for breakfast" (so confessed Mark Twain), the author apologizes for any inherited errors, omissions, or whatnot. And God forbid that the *Enterprise* had walked the straight and narrow—and dull. Its policy fit the place, fit the times.

The book's subtitle—*To Dance with the Devil*—harkens to an 1800s notion that to lust for lucre—be it gold, be it silver—was tantamount to partnering with hell's dread demon. And beware! As a hymn declared, "It's hard to dance with the Devil on your back."

The fellow on the book's cover—Adolph Sutro—was to experience this firsthand.

PROLOGUE

Devil's Gate

WHETHER BY STAGECOACH or "ankle express," frontier writer and rambler J. Ross Browne explored the nineteenth-century West—and penned droll accounts of visits to Virginia City. On his first, heading east from San Francisco, he crossed the Sierra Nevada Mountains into "the most barren, blasted and horribly desolate country that perhaps the light of heaven ever shone upon." He'd set foot in Territorial Utah, presently to become the Territory, and then the Silver State of Nevada.

On up a narrowing canyon, he encountered a rugged, rocky defile.

J. Ross Browne.

A stage bound for Virginia City.

A first sketch.

Devil's Gate, the portal to the road up to Virginia City.

In Browne's recollection:

> As I passed through the Devil's Gate it struck me that there was something ominous in the name. "Let all who enter here"—But I had already reached the other side. It was too late now for repentance. I was about to inquire where the devil—Excuse me, I use the word in no indecorous sense. I was simply about to ask where he lived, when, looking up the road, I saw a string of adventurers laden with picks, shovels, and crowbars; kegs of powder, frying pans, pitchforks—all wearily toiling in the same direction, with avarice imprinted upon their furrowed brows: the young and the old; the strong and the weak, all alike burning with an unhallowed lust for lucre; and then I shuddered as the truth flashed upon me that they were going straight to—Virginia City.[1]

Browne rhetorically asked, "Don't you smell brimstone?" Drunks staggered from saloons and reeled down muddy streets; every so often, swaggering desperados gunned each other down, and the occasional innocent. And all day long and throughout the night, a thundering legion of stamp mills battered silver from country rock.

1   J. Ross Browne, *A Peep at Washoe* (New York: Harper & Brothers, 1875), 82–83.

J. Ross Browne was not alone in his grim assessment. Miriam Florence Leslie, in her contemporaneous *From Gotham to Golden Gate*, wrote, "To call the place dreary, desolate, homeless, uncomfortable, and wicked is a good deal, but to call it God-forsaken is a good deal more, and in a tolerably large experience of this world's wonder, we never found a place more deserving the title than Virginia City."

Worse yet was life underground, where visitors were invited to boil an egg in the thermal waters flooding a sepulchral maze of drifts and stopes. The experience was enough to have a professional agnostic, Ralph Ingersoll, reconsider his long-standing belief in the nonexistence of hell. Hundreds of feet beneath the city, men were slabbed, horribly maimed, killed.

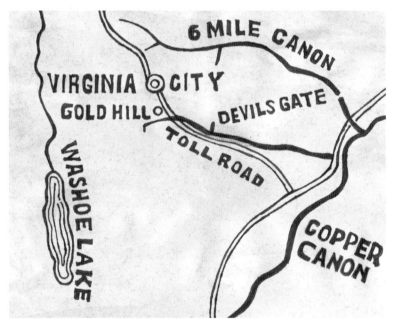

The lay of the land, from an 1860 issue of the San Francisco's *Daily Alta Californian*.

Today. Virginia City on a cold winter's night.

Slumbering C Street, once upon a time the liveliest street in the West.

Up on B Street, the courthouse was built after the old one burned to the ground.

First light on Sun Mountain, looking up from D Street and its Red Light District, once accessible from the back stairs of C Street saloons.

But it must be said that nowhere in the West were orphans so well looked after than in the Sisters of Mercy's spotless convent amidst the smoke and din of the mines.

You see, as well as misery here, there was hope. "I believe that the Almighty has created nothing in vain," wrote 1800s mining historian Charles Shinn, "and as I have passed over this awful region, the thought has fixed itself that since it is certainly useless for every other purpose, it may be a land of vast mineral wealth."

It was. In the span of a few short years, Virginia became the howling wonder of the Western Hemisphere—*and the richest place on earth*. And here, folks carved out a life for themselves and even came to revel in the place, if not love it.

Virginia City's rich ore has been long since tapped out. Gone are the days of silver kings and doughty miners, preachers and prostitutes, stockbrokers and swindlers (often one in the same).

Yet a sense of the city's eighteenth-century tumult—its high spirits and grief—remains. There are echoes of it in the wind rattling tin siding, and in the mournful howl of a lone coyote. And there is the look of the place—its shacks, its mansions, and its grand courthouse, built at the height of Virginia City's glory days. Its marble cladding glows in the early morning light. And on its facade there is a statue of Lady Justice. Across America, she was typically blindfolded, symbolic of her impartiality in weighing innocence and guilt. But not here. Better that she see for herself—and deal with—the chicanery and worse in the city at her feet, prompted by a dizzying amount of silver, at the time the most ever found, anywhere.

The devil's coin?

The look on Lady Justice's face is troubled, sad even.

To be sure, good souls walked Virginia City's streets, and deserved favorable tilts of her scales. Lady Justice appreciated

Her scales at the ready: Lady Justice, a frontier incarnation of the Roman goddess Justicia.

the city's honest citizens and innocent children, and their right to a fair shake and the protection of the law.

And aware of temptations ever-present, abounding, she couldn't help having an understanding eye for the scoundrels.

Even the scoundrels.

Left: Nevada in the early 1900s, as a fifty-year rush for riches drew to a close. Of the map's scattered settlements, two-thirds are mining camps, with the richest being Virginia City and adjoining Gold Hill.

The territory of these towns—marked by a little blue box—was mapped in detail by the Topographic Engineers of the U.S. Government's 1867–1869 40th Parallel Survey (to be recounted in the chapter entitled "The Honest Miner").

Opposite: A geological portrait of the mining district within the little box. Look closely at the sliver of white—a tiny slice of an already small area. It is marked "Comstock Lode."

Akin to a needle in a haystack, here lay, before or since, the world's richest deposit of gold and silver—cause for gunplay and mayhem, for fortunes beyond imagining.

But not for awhile, not just yet.

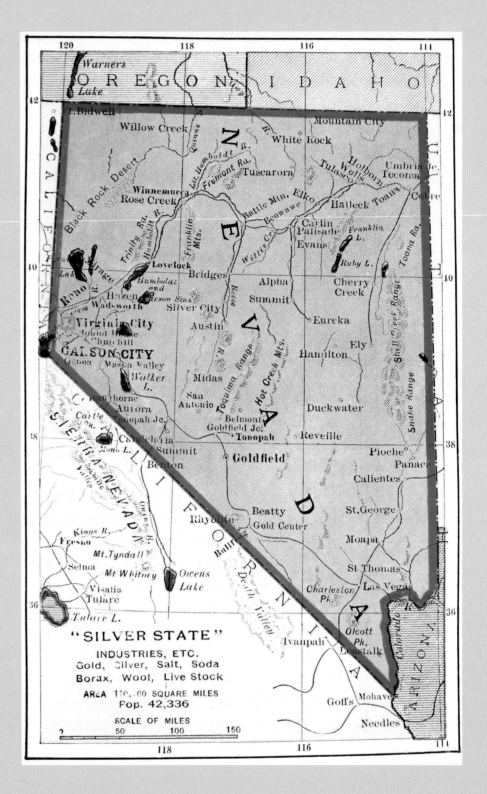

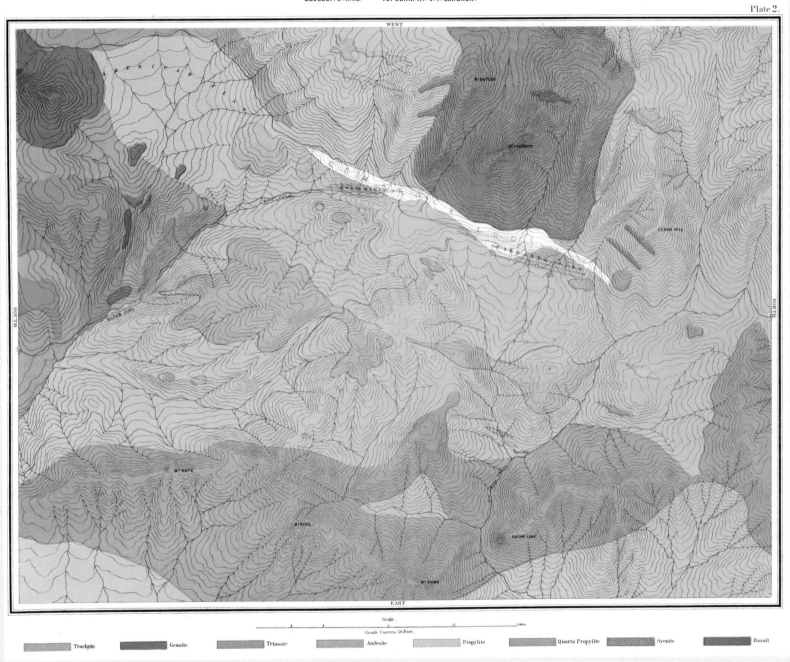

GEOLOGICAL MAP OF THE WASHOE MINING DISTRICT.

GEOLOGY: C. KING.   TOPOGRAPHY: J. T. GARDNER.

Plate 2.

Scale .

Grade Curves 50 Feet.

Trachyte   Granite   Triassic   Andesite   Propylite   Quartz Propylite   Syenite   Basalt

Fools *of* Fortune

In the early 1850s, the Almighty had yet to smile upon and bless the western reach of the Utah Territory. It was a land of rack-ribbed coyotes, the realm of a "few crows beating the air with heavy wings in their low flight above the bleak stretches of sage bush, only adding to the desolation of the scene."[2]

Yet wayfarers tarried here.

Who and for what purpose?

In a word: *gold*. Not all that much, but enough to get by.

Here is where emigrants bound for California's Mother Lode spied the snow-clad Sierra Nevadas—and forfeited their hope for untold riches. The range was daunting; moreover, here they encountered a bedraggled column trudging back east, homeward-bound, beaten and broken, dreams dashed.

Both groups—coming and going—were to pitch tents in the vicinity of the declivity known as Devil's Gate, for here an old riverbed yielded passable amounts of gold dust, even the occasional nugget (certified with a chomp of the molars to ascertain it was malleable not brittle, as was fool's gold). A camp sprung up—Johntown. By all accounts it was a bustling, cheerful place, as with mining long toms and rockers, men sifted heavier gold from lighter sands, and on a good day could make $5, even $10, and eat and sleep at Eilley Orrem's boarding house. Hailing from the highlands of Scotland, Eilley was part

2 Eliot Lord, *Comstock Mining and Mines* (Washington, DC: U.S. Geological Survey, vol. IV, 1883), 8.

In the sere, sagebrush hills of western Nevada, an overbearing H.T.P. Comstock disputes the ownership of a claim. No one had a glimmer of what would become of it.

motherly presence, part bonnie desert belle. She was renowned for her nightly serving of pork and beans.

Johntown had its characters. James Fennimore, better known as "Old Virginny" in a nod to his home state, was "feather-brained and bibulous." He scraped just enough "color" (gold) from the riffles of his rocker to keep him in drink, all the while complaining about "blue stuff"—an unknown gunk clogging his rocker and dimming his prospects.

And there was H.T.P. Comstock, better known as "Old Pancake." As he sought his fortune, he was too busy to cook anything but pancakes for breakfast, pancakes for lunch, and pancakes for dinner. It was generally believed that he was "a little cracked" in his "upper story," a suspicion confirmed by the fact that he drank little. (What sane prospector didn't drink?) Old Pancake was oft seen gazing beyond Devil's Gate, on up newly-christened Gold Canyon,

dreaming that where there's some color, there's got to be more of it. Buried perhaps.

As more wayfarers drifted into Johntown, enterprises were established, in the spirit that "miners mine gold, and merchants mine miners." A grocery tent offered produce from the nearby Carson Valley; Jacob Job opened a mercantile; and "Dutch Nick" Ambrose stocked the inevitable saloon, where on a Saturday night there was a "Grand Ball," marked by folks hollering themselves hoarse and splintering a split-log floor with their hobnail boots. A favorite dance was the "French Four," initially a problem in that it required four men and four women to make up a set—and there were but three white women in Johntown. This was solved by entreating Winnemucca, chief of the region's Paiutes, for the loan of his daughter Sarah.

There were breaks in the Saturday night revelry to toast their rosy future, even as it was increasingly shaky as Johntowners hit

Johntown, a scattering of tents and cabins in a rare stand of weather-beaten pines. Note the sole woman—possibly boarding house proprietor Eilley Orrum.

"Old Virginny."

"Old Pancake."

Miss Sarah Winnemucca.

bedrock and exhausted gold-laced sands. But then, they'd brighten as they downed "tarantula juice," a fermented potato-cinnabar concoction powerful enough to kill said spiders. Thereupon, try as they may, they'd find Jacob Job's Faro gaming layout a losing proposition. Jacob had no use for the game's traditional tin dealing box; he preferred to deal "out of hand," with players oblivious as to the opportunities this offered for sundry slippery sleights.

No matter how the pasteboards turned, the little company danced on, no matter how little they won or how much they lost. To restock their poke, they'd be back at their long toms and rockers tomorrow, grousing, as was their wont, about the unidentified "blue stuff" gumming up their works.

They were a rough-hewn, ragged, confabulating, mostly illiterate lot—with absolutely no idea that they were poised at a turning point in the fortunes of the Far West. They were oblivious to what was under their noses, hidden in plain sight. And for this, they'd be decried as "these fools of fortune."[3]

They danced on. Their leaping, twirling shadows ghosted the crudely-plastered walls of the little saloon in a desert wilderness. To the scratch of a single-fiddle orchestra, their stomps and shouts echoed up Gold Canyon, beyond Devil's Gate.

Where the ruckus was out of earshot, a light flickered in a

3   Charles Shinn, *The Story of the Mine* (New York: D. Appleton Co., 1910), 44.

The brothers Grosh.

yellowed stone cabin. Within, two brothers leafed through weighty scientific treatises, and tinkered with arcane chemical apparatuses. Ethan Allen and Hosea Grosh were sons of a New England preacher. They were a sociable enough pair, and they might well have joined the Johntowners weekly revel had they not been obsessed with understanding their canyon's geology and mineralogy.

They reasoned that the gold recovered on down the canyon didn't waft in on the wind, but rather had its origin in a source—a vein—eroded by millennia of flash floods. Accordingly, they prospected on up the canyon, on a windswept plateau known as American Flats. They sought telltale "float," gold dust pointing the way to where gold-bearing quartz broke the surface as an outcrop, or if buried, could be uncovered by test pits. And back at their cabin they had the sense to test potential ore for not only gold, but for lead, antimony, and silver.

As they'd hoped and prayed, the day came when, expectantly rushing back to their cabin, they ran a crude assay. It was cause for Allen to take quill in hand and in miniscule script (conserving paper) write their father:

> We found two veins of silver at the forks of Gold Canyon
> . . . . One of these veins is a perfect monster—

Not gold, but *silver*, flushed from ground-up ore with nitric acid.

For a time, heavy snow and a frozen rocker daunted further exploration. Then on June 8, 1857, Allen was to write:

> The rock of the vein looks very beautiful, is very soft, and will work remarkably easy. The show of metallic silver produced by exploding it in damp gunpowder is very

Allen Grosh's letter of June 8, 1857.

promising. . . . Its colors are violet-blue, blue-black, and greenish-black.

Two months later, in a next letter, the brothers' hopes were confirmed by the report of a commercial assayer off in California.

Our first assay was one-half ounce of rock: the result was $3,500 of silver to the ton, which was altogether too much of a good thing. . . . We are very sanguine of ultimate success.

But alas, three days later, Hosea Grosh accidentally impaled his foot with a pick. The wound was deep, painful, and soon gangrenous. Two weeks and he died of blood poisoning.

Allen was heartbroken, yet determined to fulfill the brothers' dream. The following November, he set out to raise funds from interests in California's Mother Lode, and was overtaken by a Sierra Nevada ice storm that had him crawling on his hands and knees, his bloodshot eyes "closing from overmastering faintness." But then, there was the bark of a dog and a blurred wisp of smoke from a cabin's chimney.

Allen was rescued, only to fade and die in a mountain mining camp—named the Last Chance.

BACK AT AMERICAN FLATS, Allen had left the brothers' cabin in the care of irascible H.T.P. Comstock, "Old Pancake." Puzzling their retorts and dog-eared volumes, he believed the brothers were on to something, but he knew not what. He then elected not to trouble himself with digging and panning, but instead kept a sly eye out for what other prospectors, drifting up from Johntown (its fortunes seriously sagging) might or might not be on to. He and his pony rambled the region, and on June 12, 1858, happened upon two or three Irish prospectors clearing their rockers of the day's sludge, and rather pleased with themselves. Without a word, Old Pancake sprang from his mount, that he might—uninvited—run his fingers through their freshly sifted earth. In the light of the setting sun, golden spangles clung to his fingers.

At length, he rose to his feet—to coolly inform the Irishmen that they were trespassing on his land. They were dumbfounded as Old Pancake imperiously explained that he had taken up a tract of a hundred and sixty acres with the intent of running cattle. (No matter that there was little or no feed.) Old Pancake was willing, however, to allow the Irishmen to continue their work, that is, if they cut him in on their claim.

Old Pancake states his terms.

About this time, the smug rascal — Old Pancake, H.T.P. Comstock — had his picture taken.

It was a preposterous proposal. He had no title to the land; there was no record of his locating a ranch. Yet he carried on so long and so sanctimoniously and so loud-mouthed that, in the interest of peace, the Irishmen shrugged and acceded to his demand.

They'd struck it rich—on what would prove to be an extension of the vein discovered by the ill-fated Grosh brothers. And for bullying, blustering Old Pancake, what better name for the discovery than, well, his own?

It would be *the Comstock Lode.*

The Johntown crowd was soon up the hill, staking claims, carousing in Dutch Nick's relocated saloon, and feverishly working their rockers. Here, as before, Old Virginny cursed the wretched blue stuff that was carrying off the quicksilver meant to amalgamate his gold. And a full year would pass before it occurred to

someone—a visiting rancher, Augustus Harrison—to question what the blue stuff actually was, so that it might be efficiently dealt with. Off in Grass Valley, California, he had a fistful of it assayed.

It was a decomposed mass of a mix of chloride of silver and silver sulphurets. Per ton, the assay report read, the stuff would yield $876 in gold—and an unexpected, astounding $3,000 in silver!

There was jubilation when the news reached the hill beyond Devil's Gate.

Then: what to name its as-yet sketchy settlement? "Pleasant Hills" was proposed, but didn't stick, for the only thing pleasant about the place was the prospect of making a pile and spending it somewhere else. "Ophir Diggings" was better and popular for a time; in the Good Book, Ophir was where King Solomon got his gold.

But then came a night recalled by Old Virginny:

Virginia City is so named.

Well, we all had a liking for whiskey, and going along, we got into a dispute about the name of the contemplated city—all of us a little sprung. The dispute was waxing warm, when an unlucky boulder happened in my way, and over it I stumbled, and away went the bottle, whiskey and I. That settled the question![4]

Staggering to his feet, Old Virginny emptied his broken bottle of its remaining liquor, and with theatrical élan proclaimed, "I baptize this ground Virginia."

So it was that Virginia City and its Comstock Lode honored two of its fools of fortune.

As one might suspect, a flurry of activity followed, but not all that much. There was, in fact, an exodus of prospectors who would as soon look for "the next big thing" rather than dig in the dirt—and to drink, not toil. As well, it was their experience that rich showings could peter out a few feet down, as at Johntown. They expeditiously (they thought) sold off their shares, with, for one, original locator Alva Gould pocketing $450 from a greenhorn from San Francisco, and drunkenly shouting to the hills, "Oh, I fooled the Californian!" Within a year, all but one of the discoverers of the Comstock lode had cashed out, with a number soon to come to a bad end. Old Virginny reportedly sold his stake to Old Pancake for "an old horse worth about $0 and a few dollars in cash," and on a subsequent drunken spree, was thrown from said stone-blind horse and killed. Old Pancake garnered a tidy $11,000, only to drift north, where an acquaintance reported, "Yes, I have seen him. He is dead now, got broke up in Montana . . . bad luck all the time . . . got crazy . . . shot himself in the head with a pistol."

Which left Virginia City bereft of its original cast—"these fools of fortune"—and ripe for new players to tramp its boards.

At which point an inquiring Englishman, marked by a brace of mutton-chop whiskers and burning eyes, rode into town from

4   As recalled by Old Virginny acquaintance Almarin B. Paul, cited in Michael J. Mackley, *John Mackay* (Reno, NV: University of Nevada Press , 2009), 17.

Captain Richard Francis Burton.

Salt Lake City. In a wildly adventurous life, Capt. Richard Francis Burton had investigated deviant sexual practices in India, bluffed his way into the holy city of Mecca, and sought the source of the Nile. In America to see what the Mormons were all about, he had happened upon this corner of their Utah Territory, but now failed to find all that much of note. It could well be that in his eyes, Virginia City but was meteor in the night, a flash of excitement destined for oblivion. He did, however, sketch the place, the source of an etching in his book, *The City of the Saints.*

Two days, and Burton saw what there was to see—which really wasn't all that much—and was on his way, unaware that his bucolic image would be the sole on-the-spot rendering of a fleeting calm before the flash and thunderation of a mighty storm.

In Burton's rendering, this is unmistakably Virginia City, identified by Sugarloaf Peak (center distance). With no sign of mining, the place is yet to become a roaring camp.

HO, *for* WASHOE!

SOFTLY, GOOD FRIENDS!

What rumor is this? Whence comes these silvery strains that are wafted to our ears from the passes of the Sierra Nevada? What dulcet Aeolian harmonies?

As I live, it is the cry of Silver! Not gold now you silly men. . . . But Silver—solid, pure SILVER! Beds of it ten thousand feet deep! Acres of it!—miles of it!—hundreds of millions of dollars poking their back up out of the earth ready to be pocketed.

Borne on the wings of the wind from the Sierra Nevada. . . . What man of enterprise could resist it? The Comstock lead!—indicating in trumpet tones the high road to fortune! [5]

So wrote adventurer J. Ross Browne, his account highlighted by wry, lively illustrations in his own hand, as he was swept up in a conglomeration of outsiders supplanting Virginia City's original rag-tag band.

Such a bedlam . . . dapper looking gentlemen mounted on fancy horses; women in men's clothes mounted on mules; whisky peddlers, stopping now and then to quench the thirst of the toiling multitude; organ grinders; riding, raving drovers, tearing frantically through the brush after self-willed cattle . . . in short, every

5 J. Ross Browne, *A Peep at Washoe,* 32–33, 36, 50–51.

Crossing the Sierra Nevadas: "An almost continuous string stretched like a giant snake dragging its slow length as far as the eye could reach." (J. Ross Browne)

Honest miner.

"Indications, sure!"

Croppings.

imaginable class and every possible species of industry was represented in this moving pageant—all stark mad for silver.

Passing through Devil's Gate, they followed the track up Gold Canyon and over a divide to Virginia City, where they fanned out to seek their fortune in a region named for its Indians (soon to be dispossessed)—Washoe! They battered the landscape with picks, pondered and puzzled what ran through their fingers, and searched anew. If at all successful—or even suspicious of what they'd found, they staked claims, pitched tents, and had at the business of mining. Six feet down, Browne sketched two miners "double jacking" a

drill bit. When their bore hole was driven to a depth of six to eight feet, they'd trade places and laboriously drill a half dozen or more additional holes, then pack the lot with black powder (in the barrel to the left). They'd then tamp in blasting caps (behind the fellow to the right's feet) connected to lengths of fuses (center bottom).

With a cry of "Fire in the hole!" they'd scramble to the surface, clap their hands to their ears, and a minute or so later, witness tons of rock flying from the earth.

Deeper on down, a strike of a match and a lit fuse would inspire a mad dash down a drift (tunnel), hoping that the fuse wasn't a defective "runner." If so, it would burn its length in seconds, not minutes.

Double jacking.

Preparing to sink a shaft, three miners pry its intended location clear of boulders. Two more wrestle a crown wheel to top a gallows frame, yet to be hammered-up. This may be where J. Ross Browne pitched his tent.

Surprise!

gathering information as to where, with little effort, they stood to stake a profitable claim. As Browne noted, "everybody had some grand secret, and the name of the game of 'dodge' and 'pump' was universally played."

There was much at stake. An assay of the time stated that a ton of the once-despised "blue stuff" was worth $1,579 in gold and $4,791 in silver![6]

That did it! No longer was Virginia City reached by foot or atop a mule or horse. Stage lines rattled through Devil's Gate at a breakneck pace, and with a shifting clientele: not so many "honest miners." Instead, a surfeit of "the floating scum of the California mining camps."

Gamblers, confidence men, harlots, the odd desperado.

6   In today's dollars, as much as $200,000.

Assay office.

As J. Ross Browne saw first hand,

> The life of the miner is one of labor, peril, and exposure, but it possesses the fascinating element of liberty, and the promise of unlimited reward. In the midst of privations amounting, at times, to the verge of starvation, what glowing visions fill the mind of the toiling adventurer!

Two pioneering assay offices were crammed with hopefuls, not only men with ore to be sampled, but loungers and hangers-on

"Silver, certain, sir!"

The rush continues.
A stage packed to its limit.

A buckboard stocked with drifters and drunks.

From across the way, the place was reasonably orderly. Close in, there was a hodge-podge of—

> Frame shanties, pitched together as if by accident; tents of canvass, of blankets, of brush, of potato sacks and old shirts, with empty whisky barrels for chimneys, smoky hovels of mud and stone; coyote holes in the mountainside.
>
> To say that their occupants were rough, muddy, unkempt and unwashed, would be but faintly expressive of their actual appearance.[7]

But, ah, fortune abounded! And top-hatted, pince-nezed speculators could cut themselves in for a song. Or so they thought.

J. Ross Browne swears he read an advertisement:

> The undersigned is prepared to sell at reasonable prices valuable claims in the following companies:
>
> *The Dead Broke, the Fool Hardy, the Love's Despair,*
> *the Grab Game, the Ragged End.*

7 *A Peep at Washoe,* 84.

Presently, the Great Monarch is, well, just a notice.

And over here there isn't much more—but oh, the promise!

J. Ross Browne's early Virginia City.

In truth, there were a trio of mines named the *Fool Catcher Nos. 1, 2, & 3.* And there was indeed a *Fly by Night Gold & Silver Mining Company.*

Alas, the land's rightful occupants were relegated to brush huts downhill from Virginia, and ill-treated. They were fated to gamble, drink, and dwell in poverty—as uphill, miner's tents and rude hovels gave way to imposing, many-storied buildings.

And all was commerce, prosperity—and a measure of mayhem.

There was an inclination to disorder, to violence even, in the city's streets and saloons. Toughs vied to become "chiefs," the likes of the notorious Sam Brown who, taking offense at a remark at a bar, cut a man's throat, then clambered onto a pool table for an afternoon nap.

Running him off.

Paiute women.

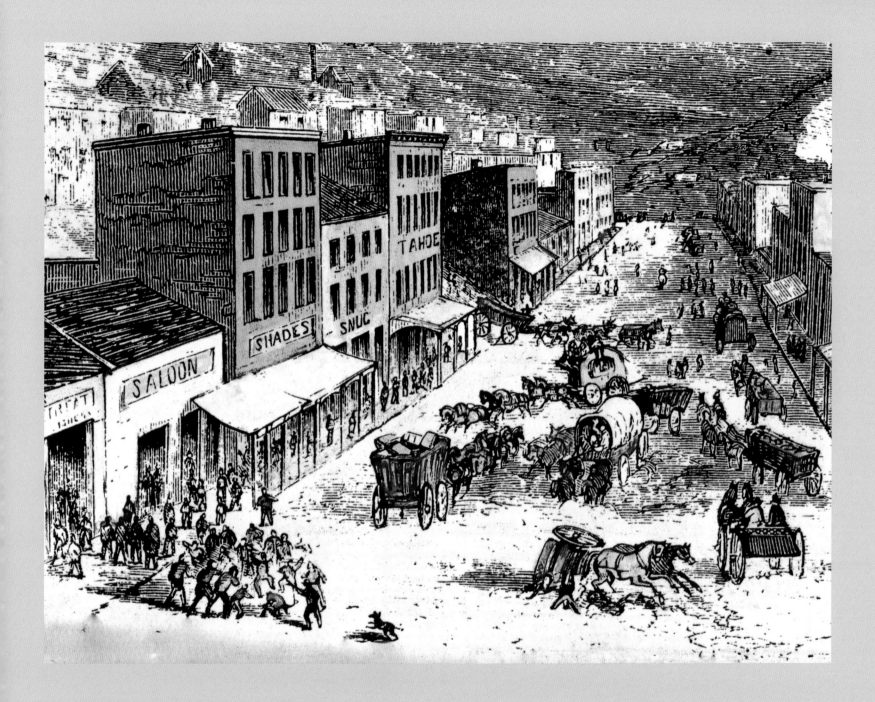

Down C Street: an overturned carriage and a wagon jam. To the left, there's a crowd
attracted to a fight, whether of dogs or two-legged toughs it's unclear.

No one dared call him out.

That is, until he took a shot or two at Henry Van Sikles, an innkeeper on the road to Virginia City, and galloped on his way. Uncowed, the innkeeper seized a double barreled fowling piece and primed it with heavy shot. In hot pursuit, he caught up with Sam Brown and with the words, "Now I kills you," lined him with lead. The verdict of a grateful coroner's jury: "Samuel Brown has come to his death from the just dispensation of an all-wise Providence. . . . It served him right."

To early observers, a human tilt toward violence had a mirror in the place's weather, in particular its "Washoe Zephyr." a westerly gale . . .

. . . in the shape of whirlwinds of from eighty to two hundred horse-power. A breeze of this kind will snatch a man's hat off his head and take it vertically a hundred feet in the air; then as he stands gazing after it, the hat suddenly comes down at his feet, completely flattened as though it had been struck with a sledge hammer.

The Zephyr filled the air with rags, empty cans, bottles, crowbars, pickaxes, cooking stoves, cats and Indian babies. . . . "Sleep! Sleep no more!" The zephyr doth murder sleep.[8]

8 Dan De Quille, *The Big Bonanza* (New York: Alfred A. Knopf, 1947), 187–188.

The Washoe Zephyr — ripping off tin roofs and lofting donkeys.

Solace-offering hurdy-gurdy girls.

There is a certain delight in this escalation of imagery—from a wafted hat to airborne donkeys—that was to become endemic in Virginia City. Its populace fancied excitement, be it real or imaginary.

Why brave such weather, Virginians asked, when they were blessed with saloons on the order of the Cosy Home, the Miner's Retreat, and the Fancy Free. And within same, there were the blandishments of hurdy-gurdy girls (named for a stridulous cousin of the accordion), who offered song, dance, and liquid refreshment out front, and "horizontal refreshment" in little rooms down the hall or in shanties out back.

Here, other than drink and cards, was the city's first entertainment.

"A Question of Title."

A patched-pants fellow
who's had his fill.

Then by day, a miner was back to his hammer, drill, and keg of black powder. And as J. Ross Browne witnessed, there was the occasional dispute of a mining claim.

The chaos of the place aside, the mines of Virginia City were staggeringly productive, with due credit to a treasure-fueled work ethic. Hundreds of teams and thousands of animals freighted in supplies—to head out laden with silver ore.

A year of all this, and the time came for raconteur Browne to be on his way down the mountain and return to a calmer if duller world beyond Devil's Gate.

He was in awe of what he'd seen and experienced:

The hillsides, for a distance of more than a mile, are perfectly honeycombed. Steam engines are puffing their steam, smokestacks are blackening the air; quartz batteries are battering; subterranean blasts are bursting up the earth . . . saloons are glittering with their gaudy bars and fancy glasses, and many colored liquors, and thirsty men are swilling the burning poison, hurdy-gurdy girls are singing bacchanalian songs in bacchanalian dens . . . All is life, excitement, avarice, lust, deviltry and enterprise. A strange city truly, abounding in strange exhibitions and startling combinations of the human passions.

Where on earth is there such another place?[9]

———

As J. Ross Browne took his leave, he may well have crossed paths with a black slave who'd been granted his freedom, the courtly Grafton T. Brown. Both were artists. Whereas J. Ross captured the

9 J. Ross Browne, *Washoe Revisited* (Gloucester, MA: Folly Cove, n.d.), 151.

Tons and tons and tons of silver, beyond imagining.

boisterous hurly-burly of the place, Grafton T. would convey its promise. Making the rounds of the city's enterprises, he was well received as he solicited funds to create a grand aerial panorama, a portrait of a camp-become-city, a city now with a shift to order and civility.

In his mind's eye, he took wing as would a raven, and hovered in the sky.

With astounding accuracy, Brown detailed every structure on Virginia's rise to Sun Mountain, and with a subtle sense of shading, lent the scene a dramatic sense of depth. On close inspection, B Street appears a busy thoroughfare—that would soon to cede importance to C Street. (Note its Volunteer Fire Department barn.) On down the hill, there's D Street, scattered with one and two room red-light cribs—and behold!, a church, either that of Catholic Father Hugh Gallager or the Methodist Reverend Jesse L. Bennet, whose sermons were "answered with heaps of gold and silver." It is hard to say which it was; both churches were flattened by a Washoe Zephyr.

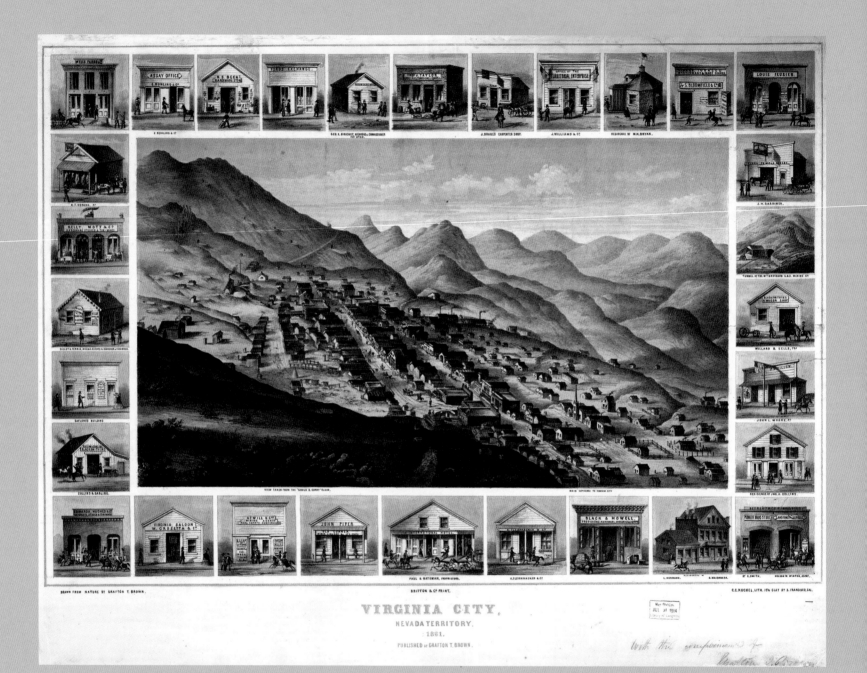

Grafton T. Brown's 1861 "bird's-eye" view of Virginia City.

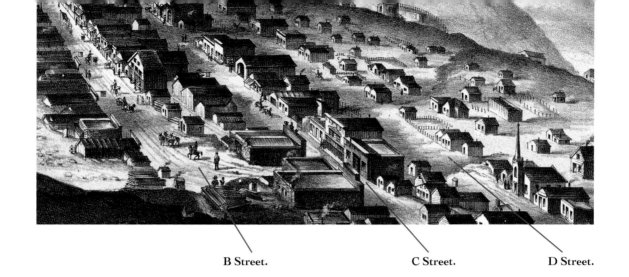

B Street.   C Street.   D Street.

Advertising Grafton T. Brown's sponsors, the borders of the view offer a sampling of Virginia's early businesses.

In November of 1860, a first newspaper, the *Enterprise*, was moved lock, stock, and barrel from the territorial capital of Carson City, and in the words of reporter Dan De Quille, "was a queerly arranged establishment." Out back,

> The proprietors had fitted up a shed as a kitchen and din-
> ing- and lodging-place. Bunks were ranged around the sides
> of the room one above the other, as on shipboard, and here editors, printers, proprietors, and all hands "bunked" after the style of miners in their cabins. A Chinaman, "Old Joe," did the cooking, and three times each day the whole crowd of "newspaper men" were called out to the long table in the shed to get their "square meal." The "printer's devil" went for numerous lunches between meals, and often came flying out into the composition-room with a large piece of pie in his mouth, and the old Chinaman at his heels.[10]

10 *The Big Bonanza*, 157.

Grosetta's saloon.

Mining supplies.

Piper's saloon.

The International Hotel.

Joe Goodman, portly and affable, was the captain of this little ship, and was determined that its reporters not put on airs, but to deliver copy that was clear, lively, and if called for, irreverent. Just the thing for "the boys," the city's oft-rowdy miners. Shifting from a weekly to a daily, the *Enterprise* prospered. And in May of 1863, Joe Goodman scratched his head. In the day's mail he had received, unsolicited, a humorous sketch written by one "Josh," a

The *Territorial Enterprise.* With, out front, a ragamuffin peddling a copy.

Josh's dream of western adventure.

gold-seeker in the remote camp of Aurora, off to the north. Reading it, he smiled, even laughed aloud. The fellow, whoever he was, was good, if a bit cockeyed.

———⚬———

IN AURORA, said Josh was living out a dream—or at least he hoped he was.

As a boy back in Missouri, he and his brother had witnessed gold seekers rushing through their quiet town and hastening west. "Ho, for California!" The boys played at digging and panning gold worth "half a dollar a day at first, two or three times as much, later, and by and by whole fortunes, as our imaginations became inured to the work."

Fifteen years had passed; he was a grown man and had ventured west, with a glint in his eye for not only gold, but for tramping and experiencing frontier America.

Wagon trains, Sierra cascades, Indians and buffalos. He'd see it all. Even strike it rich!

JOSH *and* JULIA

HERE NOW IS A CHRONICLE of parallel lives—of two souls who sought their fortunes in Virginia and, even though they may never had met, were star-crossed in their chosen pursuits, one for the better, one for the worst.

IN 1862, OVER IN WEAVERVILLE, California, Julia, her last name Smith, maybe not, was doing well though not that well, as an "accommodating woman" servicing a variety of gents—tradesmen, the occasional banker, farm and ranch hands. She drempt of a better life. Her calling would be the same, that of a prostitute, but the stakes, they could be higher.

Off on its rich, windy hill, Virginia City beckoned.

THAT SAME YEAR, up in Aurora, Nevada, Josh was down on his luck. After several years of "variegated vagabonding," he was yet to strike it rich, or even hold down a decent job. He was broke; he was blue. He'd persisted, though, in dispatching sketches to the *Territorial Enterprise*, and huzzah! in September he'd received a letter offering him a job filling in for reporter Dan De Quille, who'd requested a leave to visit kin back East. The pay: twenty-five dollars a week.

Unable to afford passage on a stage, Josh had little choice to take the "ankle express" ninety miles to Virginia City. The going was hot, dry. He trudged on by the light of the moon; he slept on the haystacks of ranches along the way.

BIRDS EYE VIEW OF

VIRGINIA CITY

STOREY COUNTY, NEVADA.

1875

1 COURT HOUSE.	9 CITY CEMETERY.
2 PUBLIC SCHOOL.	14 ODD FELLOWS BUILDING.
3 " "	15 MASONIC "
4 " "	16 PIONEER'S HALL.
5 CONGREGATIONAL CHURCH.	17 INTERNATIONAL HOTEL.
6 METHODIST EPISCOPAL "	18 PIPER'S OPERA HOUSE.
7 ROMAN CATHOLIC "	19 WASHOE CLUB.
8 EPISCOPAL "	20 BANK OF CALIF'T
9 1ST BAPTIST "	21 WELLS FARGO & CO. EXPRESS BUILT
10 ST MARY'S CONVENT.	22 VIRGINIA & TRUCKEE R.R. PAS'T DEPOT.
11 MASONIC CEMETERY.	23 " " " FREIGHT "
12 ODD FELLOWS "	24 MONT DAVIDSON LIBERTY POLE ERECTED BY EAGLE ENG'E CO. N° 3.
25 MARY'S SHAFT	36 MARIPOSA M.N'T CO'S WORKS.
26 ADV. PLANING MILLS.	37 CALIFORNIA " " "
27 UNION FOUNDRY.	38 CHAR & CURRY " " "
28 " "	39 SAVAGE " " "
29 SUNDAY BOILER WORKS.	40 HALE & NORCROSS " " "
30 VIRGINIA CITY GAS	41 " " "
31 CON. VIRGINIA M.N'T CO	42 CHOLLAR POTOSI " " "
32 CONSOLIDATED MILL	43 MINT
33 OPHIR MINING CO. "	44 SENATOR " " "
34 SIERRA NEVADA "	45 BULLION " " "
35 "	46 ANDES " " "

A bird's-eye view by artist Augustine Koch. It is a stage set for the Virginia City life and times of Josh and Julia.

The composing room of the *Territorial Enterprise,* relocated from A to C Street.

Arriving in Virginia and shambling into the *Enterprise's* office, "Josh" proclaimed, "My name is Clemens, and I've come to write for the paper." Editor Joe Goodman didn't quite know what to make of the disheveled, gimlet-eyed fellow with bushy red hair. But any doubts soon acceded to delight. The man's reporting was just the ticket for Virginia's salt-of-the-earth populace. Wry, imaginative, a good read. If anything, Josh's articles were a bit on the reckless side, with a growing indifference to news as news. Why not? Give the place what it gave: ruckus, scoundrelry, gunplay! Intrigued by the town's casual violence, Josh was to make light of it. He signed off a letter back east:

P.S.—I have just heard five pistol shots down the street—and as such things are in my line, I will go and see about it. P.S. No 2—The pistol did its work well—one man—a Jackson County Missourian, shot two of my friends (police officers) through the heart—both died within three minutes. To bed at sunrise. Up again at noon.

Did this really happen? Or did the likes of this add a dash of color to uneventful, slow days? Be this as it may, Josh thrived. He loved the *Enterprise,* slept on its ink-and-tobacco-splattered floor, and enjoyed carousing with the paper's staffers, especially recently returned Dan De Quille.

That wasn't Dan's real name; it was William Wright. He as well had signed articles "Ebenezer Queerkut" and "Picaroon Pax." And this got Josh to thinking; reinvention was a Virginia sport, so why not join the game? His real name was Sam Clemens, but writing a letter to the editor back in Hannibal, Missouri, he'd used the pseudonym "Thomas Jefferson Snodgrass," then up in Aurora, "Josh." Now, he heeded of his frequent call to barkeeps at John Piper's Saloon. Having bought drinks for himself and a pal, he'd instruct them to write "Mark Twain" on the establishment's back-bar chalkboard.

Josh, now Mark Twain, so signed a February 2, 1863, *Territorial* article, and stuck with the name.[11]

Josh, now Mark.

COME EARLY APRIL of 1863, an inbound stage reigned up, and out stepped a tall, slim, attractive woman, no longer Julia Smith, but rather Julia Bulette, a name redolent of romance (if of an eve) and good times (if fleeting).[12] She canvassed Virginia's Red Light District, and settled on a two-room, comfortable cottage at 4 North D Street. She furnished it with the best she could afford: a carved black walnut sofa and four matched chairs, Brussels carpeting, the inevitable spittoon. Her bedroom, darkened by damask curtains, boasted a huge mahogany bed, with a plain white spread in summertime, and a fancy wool one for winter nights. There was no plumbing, no kitchen. She took her meals next door, prepared by sister harlot Gertrude Holmes. She hired a Chinaman to, every morning, stoke her fire and clear up the ephemera of a night's revelry.

By all accounts, Julia was kind and considerate, and may even have nursed injured or sick miners.

Among others of high and low estate, Julia befriended dashing Tom Peasley, proprietor of the popular Sazerac Saloon, and Chief of Virginia's Engine Company No 1. She was frequently at the station, and may well have lent a hand putting out fires, or at least offering

Julia Bulette.

11 There are conflicting explanations of "Mark Twain." It could have been a sailor's call as he sounded the depth of the Mississippi River navigated by a steamboat.
12 Mark Twain's stint in Virginia City is well documented; Julia Bulette's not so. Though April of 1863 is her most likely time of arrival, conflicting (dubious) reports have her in Virginia City as early as 1859.

Written on the image's back: "Julia's House, Virginia City." (Maybe so; probably not.)

Mark Twain's desk.

34

coffee and cake to the boys who were. They elected her an honorary member, proclaimed her the company's mascot.

Julia Bulette was soon the best-known—and admired, though not by all—of Virginia's "light ladies."

MARK TWAIN, AS WELL, was a name with a measure of fame, and it went to his head. He saw himself as a "prince wherever I go . . . laughing and joking," and free to write what he wished, insult who he may. But give him credit for adding, "I am proud to say I am the most conceited ass in the Territory."

And the question is raised: Might Mark and Julia have been acquainted? With the answer: probably, though not certainly, with the evidence an enlargement of the bird's-eye view at the outset of this chapter. On it, note the haunts of Mark and Julia—and their proximity in an eight-block area.

There was many a possibility for a meet-up, be it a tip of the hat and a responding smile and nod, a chat, even something more intimate. The two could have crossed paths strolling a C Street boardwalk. Both enjoyed performances at Maguire's Opera House, Mark seated up front in a "Printer's Pew" and Julia in a curtained box reserved for the fair but frail. Both were sociable. It was the essence of Julia's trade, and Mark danced a "deft quadrille."

We can assume no more as to their relationship—but instead recount what, in the same town at the same time, became of the two.

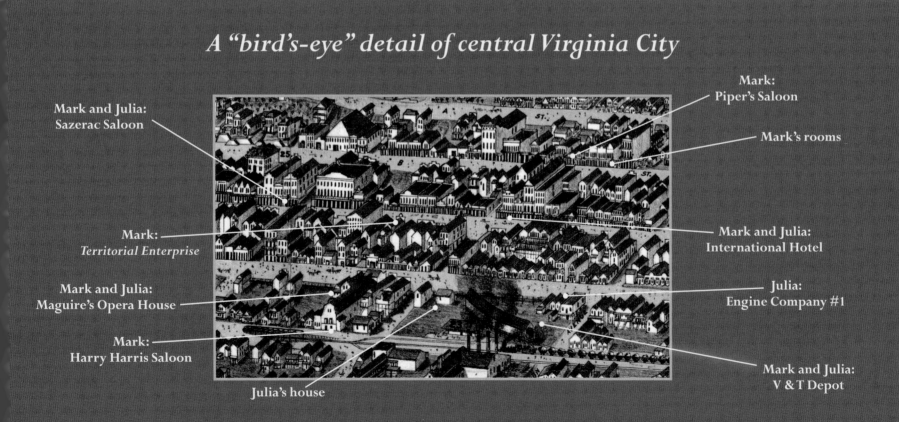

A "bird's-eye" detail of central Virginia City

Mark and Julia:
Sazerac Saloon

Mark:
Territorial Enterprise

Mark and Julia:
Maguire's Opera House

Mark:
Harry Harris Saloon

Julia's house

Mark:
Piper's Saloon

Mark's rooms

Mark and Julia:
International Hotel

Julia:
Engine Company #1

Mark and Julia:
V & T Depot

MARK FANCIED HIMSELF a man about town, after sundown a high-living habitué of theaters, saloons, and billiard halls. On a memorable eve, he and Dan De Quille took visiting humorist Artemis Ward on a tour of the city's sights and districts. They boisterously downed "blandy" (rice brandy) in E Street's Chinatown, then, sheets to the wind, headed up the hill to D Street. Coming to a row of "low frame houses" they elected to take a shortcut clambering onto a shed and then leaping from roof to roof to roof— to dance with hurdy-gurdy girls in a C Street establishment that offered both public and intimate entertainment. And drank the night away.

It's not impossible that one of those "low frame houses" was Julia's. Here, she offered leisurely evenings, often devoted to a single customer. She provided, claret to rum, a range of spirits. Whatever ailed or troubled a fellow, she listened—and offered him a genuinely good time.

This was a marked contrast to a generally seedy life up and down D Street, walked by *doves du pave* Bigmouth Annie, the Spring Chicken, the Carson Banger, and the Big Bonanza. Or Fighting Annie. Working out of the Bon Ton Saloon and annoyed at a customer, she smashed a champagne bottle over his head—to be henceforth known as a "striking beauty."

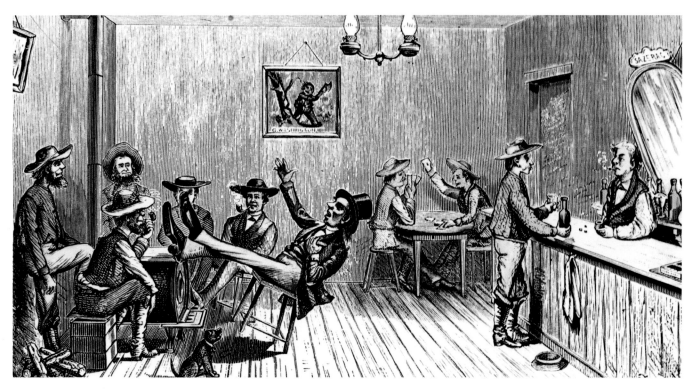

Tom Peasley's Sazerac Saloon. Mark and Julia were regulars.

Rather, the atmosphere at Julia's place—sometimes called her palace—was refined, calm, good hearted.

Many were her friends.

In July of 1864, she donned a fireman's helmet, climbed onto Engine Company No. 1's fire truck, graciously received a brass trumpet filled with French roses, and reigned as Queen of Virginia's Independence Day Parade. For the occasion, the city's streets were jammed with miners and moguls, and its buildings hung with red, white and blue bunting.

<hr />

THAT BOISTEROUS DAY, Mark Twain may well have hung from an *Enterprise* window, cheering on the parade, the fire truck, Julia. He wouldn't have missed this for the world. And that day could be taken to mark a Virginia watershed. The city's years to date had been years of hope and opportunity for all—"grand flush times"—but now, for every dream fulfilled, dozens would be dashed. With eastern syndicates tightly controlling Virginia's mines, bitterness and anger soured the common man, and wooly times were at hand: at first, drunks cursing everyone and everything; then, at the least provocation, men coming to blows, even shooting one another. Twain reported this, even gloried in this to the extent that he imagined—he *invented*—mayhem and crimes.

On October 28, 1864, accountability be damned, he went too far.

"The Empire City Massacre" reported that one Philip Hopkins had gone berserk and killed his wife and children with an axe, a knife, and a club. Two other children, Julia and Emma, were seriously injured. Hopkins then scalped and decapitated his red-headed wife, then cut his own throat. But he still managed to ride into Carson City where he "fell in dying condition in front of the Magnolia

A sole, authentic portrait of Julia Bulette.

saloon. Sheriff and citizens rode to Hopkins' house, where a ghastly scene met their gaze." In studied detail, Twain described the bloody scene.

All of this, every last detail, was feverishly fabricated—in the misbegotten belief that the article would draw attention to a San Francisco stock swindle, the alleged cause of Hopkins' rampage. Twain believed that inconsistencies in the article would give it away as a hoax and provide a good laugh for his readers. Not so. They were outraged. Virginia's *Evening Bulletin* exclaimed, "God knows our Territory has a reputation for being the theater of scenes of blood and violence that really do occur."

Even so, Mark Twain's dalliance with violence persisted—and caught up with him. Calling a rival newspaperman "an unmitigated liar and abject coward" garnered him a challenge to a duel, with pistols at fifteen paces. As Twain target practiced, the notion that his high-flown insults could kill him sunk in. There was no jest in a duel.

As the appointed hour neared, both parties were terrified—and both fled the scene, Mark to catch a westbound morning stage. And

There was an escalation of brawls, knifings, and killings.

"The age of chivalry is past."

as it bumped down the grade, he may have reflected that this was just as well. Virginia had lost its luster, was no longer the place for a dissipated, high-flying humorist. He was to write: "The seventh day I resigned."

The *Gold Hill Evening News* waved a sardonic good-bye:

> We don't wonder. Mark has indulged in the game infernal—in short, "played hell." He has vamoosed, cut stick, absquatulated.

JULIA BULETTE remained in Virginia City, and would appear to have done quite well for herself. According to latter-day *Enterprise* editor Lucius Beebe:

> Julia was prosperous. Diamonds sparkled at her throat and ears. Wells Fargo brought vintage French champagne for her table, and cut flowers, the rarest of all articles of *grand lux*, were delivered to her door every day. . . . Julia's Palace

A bandy cut-throat.

In high esteem: A man who'd killed eight men.

was the cultural center of the community. She brought airs and grace where comparative barbarism had reigned, and the miners accorded her an homage that elsewhere would have been the prerogative of a great lady.

Historian Dee Brown elaborated:

She charged $1,000 a night. With her earnings Julia was able to build a magnificent brothel in the rococo design. It was the largest and most profitable brothel in Virginia City. She staffed it with beautiful girls imported from San Francisco, and dressed them in the latest Parisian fashions. . . . Julia appeared regularly in the streets of Virginia City, clad in costly sables and jewels, driving a lacquered brougham which bore a painted Escutcheon on the panel which was four aces crowned by a lion couchant.

Others were to chime in. And for all their color and cleverness, there's a choice of words: *hokum and hooey, nonsense and balderdash.* Julia was never a madam; she had no Frisco girls. There were no cut flowers, diamonds, or glittering chandeliers. No French champagne was poured. The lacquered coach was imaginary. Here were respectable writers hoodwinking both their readers, and serially, each other—truth absquatulated.[13]

In reality, Julia worked alone, and never moved on from her modest D Street house. Day-in and day-out plying her trade, she got by, even afforded luxuries in the line of clothing and adornment.

13 Why? Was it the air in Virginia City, with historians sniffing reality and exhaling fantasy? Mark Twain was not alone in his inventions and excesses.

But now, in her mid-thirties, she didn't have much hope for her future in a rough, oft violent town. Still, she provided lonely men comfort and refinement unusual in western mining camps. She was a prostitute, but very much a kind woman.

The years slipped by: 1864, 1865, 1866.

———•◦•———

For Mark Twain, they were good years. Over in the Gold Rush country, he wrote "The Celebrated Jumping Frog of Calaveras County," his passport to national attention. He took up lecturing, and in search of new material, sojourned to the Sandwich Isles (an old name for Hawaii). On his return he fleetingly visited Virginia City, where, walking from the wings of Maguire's Opera House, he was greeted by "a hurricane of applause." Papers trumpeted "his drollest humor," his "immense success." His head held high, he was on his way the next morning, a contrast to his ignominious exit two years previously.

———•◦•———

Julia may well have attended Mark's lecture. Required to discreetly enter through a side door, she enjoyed lectures, concerts, and plays, highlights of a life that had now dealt her a bad hand. She had taken sick, the exact nature of her illness a matter between Julia and Doc Christopher Green, who'd long attended her.

Though still able to entertain customers, Julia's star was dimming.

———•◦•———

New Year's day, 1867. Mark was aboard a steamer to New York— where he strode down the gangplank intent on becoming the toast of America's Gilded Age. He wrote, "Make your mark in New York, and you are a made man." He cajoled his way into the exclusive

D Street—and Julia's walk home from Maguire's Opera House.

Century Club, its membership limited to prominent authors and artists.

***

SATURDAY EVENING, January 19, 1867. In the past week, Julia's condition had improved, and she walked south on D Street to attend a performance of *The Robber* and the farce *Willful Murder* at Maguire's Opera House.[14] But denied front-door admission and fed up with being relegated to the prostitutes' box, she left in a huff.

On her way home, she visited her long-time neighbor Gertrude Holmes, and at about 11:30 p.m. bid her goodnight. A customer was due at her cottage come midnight.

At about 5 a.m. the next morning, the man who delivered the morning edition of the *Territorial Enterprise* heard a scream down

14 The titles of the plays were an omen of what would transpire that very night.

Horrible Murder
A WOMAN STRANGLED TO DEATH IN HER BED

Blood-Curdling Tragedy
Directly in the Heart of the City

D Street, possibly from Julia's cottage. At 11 a.m. the Chinaman who Julia hired to build a fire every morning saw her snug in her bed, and took care not to disturb her. A half hour later, Gertrude stopped by to call her to breakfast—and discovered her dead. Quickly summoned, the police determined that she had been struck with a pistol, beaten with a firewood log, and smothered with a pillow. Imprints of fingers and a thumb remained on her throat. Most of her furs, jewelry, and fine clothes—her treasures of a hard life—had been stolen.

The scene echoed Mark Twain's "Empire City Massacre," except this time, it was real.

The *Enterprise* headlined:

A storm raged as a crepe-draped funeral procession wound to the Flowery Hill Cemetery: sixty members of the fire department on foot, the Metropolitan Brass Band, and finally, sixteen carriages of mourners bearing friends and the "sisterhood" of the deceased. Virginia's saloons were hung with black wreaths. As the cortege passed by, the city's respectable ladies drew their parlor curtains.

As far as is known, Mark knew little if anything of this.

In May, a break in the case came when a Mrs. Cazentre of nearby Gold Hill reported that she had bought a dress once worn by Julia. She'd purchased it from a Frenchman, Jean Marie Villain, known also as John Millian. As further evidence, there was a trunk this Millian had left in storage at the bakery where he worked. Police Chief Edwards examined its contents, and swore that Julia had worn its opera cape, its watch and the chain and the charms affixed to it. It appears he had befriended her.

A warrant was issued.

IN JUNE, Mark Twain set sail for the Holy Land on the ship *Quaker City*. He scribbled notes lampooning his sanctimonious, fuddy-duddy fellow passengers—and, once ashore, the biblical landscapes and sites they admired. He skipped the Sabbath, played cards.

IN JULY, John Millian was brought to trial, and with little ado sentenced to be hung by the neck until dead. The case was appealed to the state's Supreme Court, which ruled in favor of the jury's vote in Virginia City.

ON APRIL 24 OF THE following year, the *Enterprise* related, "He comes back to us after many wanderings by sea and land in foreign countries." The fellow in question was Mark Twain, come to lecture, come to lampoon his Holy Land adventure.

Alighting from his stagecoach, he beheld a crowd thronging Virginia's streets, a somber crowd, yet a crowd possessed by a nervous energy. It surged east, out of town, to a hammered-up gallows. There, three thousand people awaited the militia escort and the wagon bearing John Millian, and Virginia's first ever public

Execution of John Millain, for the Murder of Julia Bulette.

John Milleain.
Murderer of Jule Bulette.

(Misspelled, but the same man.)

execution. Some were stoked with vengeance, some were appalled, some had packed picnics. What Mark said to his old friends or was thinking was unknown—that is, until, a hundred and forty-six years later, the discovery of a previously-unknown dispatch to the *Chicago Republican* (May 31, 1868). He wrote:

This is the man I wanted to see hung. I joined the appointed physicians, so that I might be admitted within the charmed circle and be close to Melanie [Millian] . . .

I watched him at that sickening moment when the sheriff was fitting the noose about his neck, and pushing the knot this way and that to get it nicely adjusted, and if they had been measuring Melanie for a shirt, he could not have been more perfectly serene. I never saw anything like that before. My own suspense was almost unbearable—my blood was leaping through my veins, and my thoughts were crowding and trampling upon each other. Twenty moments to live—fifteen to live—ten to live—five—three—heaven and earth, how the time galloped!—and yet that man stood there unmoved though he knew that the sheriff was reaching deliberately for the drop while the black cap descended over his quiet face!—then down through the hole in the scaffold the strap-bound figure shot like a dart!—a dreadful shiver started at the shoulders, violently convulsed the whole body all the way down, and died away with a tense drawing of the toes downward, like a doubled fist—and all was over!

I saw it all. I took exact note of every detail, even to Melanie's considerably helping to fix the leather strap that bound his legs together and his quiet removal of his slippers—and I never wish to see it again. I can see that

DREAMS DISSIPATED.

stiff straight corpse hanging there yet, with its black pillow-cased head turned rigidly to one side, and the purple streaks creeping through the hands and driving the fleshy hue of life before them. Ugh!

With John Millian's leap into the dark, Mark Twain's and Julia Bulette's lives had finally, sadly intersected.

That night, on the stage of Maguire's Opera House, Mark Twain carried on about the Holy Land, and the next morning he left Virginia City, never to return—though, in a way, he did—in writing *Roughing It,* a transparently fictionalized account of his two years in the town. His friend William Dean Howells reviewed the book:

> The grotesque exaggeration and broad irony with which he described the life are conjecturably the truest colors that could have been used . . . an extravagant joke, *the humor of which was only deepened by its netherside to tragedy*.

A lasting, indelible image of that tragedy had to have been the execution of John Millian, and it could not have helped but influence, joking aside, *Roughing It*'s serious condemnation of frontier violence, the casual violence Twain once made light of it.

Scenarios that he has sketched in the pages of the *Territorial Enterprise* could be real, and what was real, could be terrible. "In new countries," Twain wrote, "murders breed murders."

———

WHEN, TEN YEARS EARLIER, "Josh" had set foot in Virginia City, his aspect had been that of a frontier rustic: "damaged slouch hat, blue woolen shirt, and pants crammed into boot-tops. I gloried in the absence of coat, vest, and braces. I felt rowdyish and 'bully'."

No more. Those days had come—and gone. There would be a shift to polite society and white linen suits.

His irrepressible humor, though, wasn't about to knuckle under. Rather, it would be linked to a newfound empathy for the trials and tribulations of the characters in his life, be they real or imagined. He'd turned a corner—gained a new perspective—in *Roughing It.*

He's be the wiser for it.

In Virginia, prostitution persisted—and provided a ready market for a photographer's 75-cent darkroom lantern.

The HONEST MINER

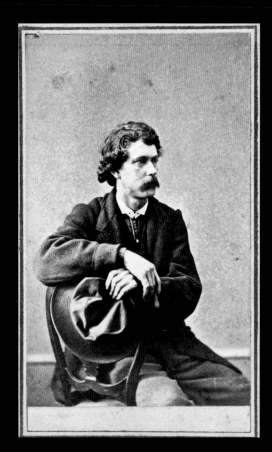

Timothy H. O'Sullivan.

In 1867, the U.S. government dispatched an expedition that would follow the 40th parallel west, that it might determine the region's potential for habitation and exploitation—with Virginia City a major point of interest.

Despite his well-known graphic images of the Civil War, the survey's photographer, Timothy H. O'Sullivan, remains an elusive figure, a widely respected artist about whom next to nothing is known. His legacy lies is his work, meticulous and creative.

Upon his crossing a desolate, waterless basin known simply as "The Great American Desert," it was a relief to follow a rutted track up into Nevada's Washoe hills, and sight not a military outpost or camp, but a *city*—a city like none other, and the closer O'Sullivan drove his wagon, the louder the shriek of mine whistles, the rumble of cages plunging deep into the earth, the throbbing of hundreds of ore stamps in dozens of mills. The racket was relentless, around the clock, all but daring a new arrival to sleep.

O'Sullivan was struck by—and recorded—the sheer industrial might of the place. And in awe of surface workings, he was curious as to what was happening below his feet, thousands of feet down.

Never before had anyone attempted to photograph this shadowy world. He was tempted to give it a try.

Positioning his view camera in the Savage mine's hoist house, he photographed men dressed for the winter's icy cold. As they descended to the mine's current working levels, they'd shuck off their overcoats as the temperature soared as high as 125 degrees Fahrenheit. O'Sullivan couldn't help but wonder: Would the sudden change crack his

Crossing the Carson sand dunes and bound for Virginia, O'Sullivan's travelling darkroom, recently a Civil War ambulance.

From the north, O'Sullivan's Virginia City.

The Gould & Curry mine and mill.

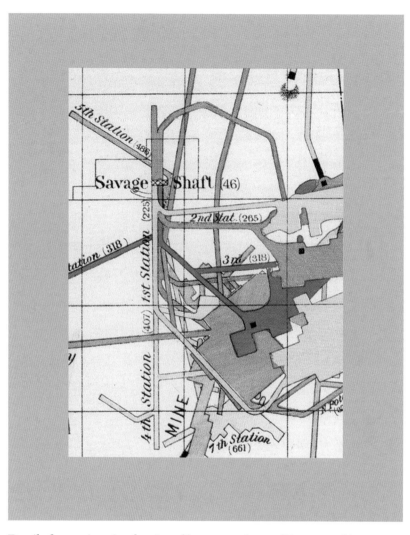

Detail of an engineering drawing of layer-upon-layer of Savage workings.

Mule trains loading ore at the Savage mine.

The Savage shaft's miners, cages, and ore cars.

lens, or at the very least fog it up? As well as heat, there'd be stifling humidity, coalescing in underground clouds.

Nothing ventured, nothing gained. Plunging 800 feet a minute, down he went.

His view camera survived, but due to its unwieldy bulk, was all but useless in the Savage's cramped, contorted drifts. But then, by good fortune, he'd brought along a small, stereoscopic camera, and could, he thought, enlarge one of its images, probably by copying it with his view camera.

He touched a match to one, then another magnesium flare, told a startled miner to freeze, uncapped his lens, and created a first-ever scene in the depths of a mine.

O'Sullivan was to ink the back of a print of this first image: "The Honest Miner."

First used in the 1849 California gold rush, the expression implies a never-tell-a-lie, doughty, dull soul. But no, that's hardly what O'Sullivan and others had in mind. Rather, they had in mind an "Honest-to-God!" miner, an individual who, as well as being skilled, might otherwise be irascible, ribald, and not above personally sampling a mine's wares.

On his way west, an Honest Miner was said to sing:

And when I get my pocket full
In that bright land of gold,
I'll have a rich and happy time:
Live merry 'til I'm old.

But once west, his tune took a bittersweet turn:

Cameras of the day: a large view camera (*top*) and a a small stereoscopic model (*bottom*). In the depths of Virginia's mines, O'Sullivan was to use both.

My fare is hard and so is my bed,
I've worked until I'm almost dead,
I ne'er shall lie in clean white sheets,
But in my blanket roll.
The girls I thought so sweet,
They think me but a fool.

The Honest Miner lived with his lot, no complaints. He was declared "the last in a long line of adventurers unto whom the delight of the new world is its newness. Sometimes his work is permanent,

but he is never quite sure. He loves to tell of the ups and downs of his own fortune, and there is no bitterness in his memory of his failures. His habitual mood is one of sober satire."[15] As when he'd posted a notice by an open shaft:

GENTLEMEN WILL PLEASE NOT FALL DOWN THE SHAFT,
FOR THERE ARE MEN AT WORK BELOW.

———•—✦—•———

OVER THE COURSE of several weeks, Timothy O'Sullivan was up and down the shafts of the Gould & Curry and Savage mines, probably taking a single photograph at a time, with a number of images, for one reason or another, dead losses. And he was accommodated by additional honest miners freezing their action for the benefit of long exposures. The images are crisp and sharp, evidence that O'Sullivan had found the space to set up his ungainly view camera.

The scenes he captured bear witness that when O'Sullivan's flares sputtered out, a lone miner worked by the light of a single candle. All but in the dark. And, no surprise, his imagination could get the better of him, fueled by the creaks and splintering of timbers and the groans and slabbing of shifting rock.

Rats scampered.

Were *Tommyknockers* afoot?

With their experience in deep tin mines, Cornishmen from England were welcome on the Comstock, though not always their unseen companions, Tommyknockers. They were described as wizened little men with long gray beard; they had "large heads, big ears

15 Samuel McChord Crothers, *The Pardoner's Wallet* (Boston: Houghton Mifflin, 1905) 182–3.

The Comstock's chloride of silver was often crumbly, easily worked.

An eerie image of a cave-in—including the foot of a miner, working on.

Undercutting an overhang, a miner at risk.

A final underground image. At first glance, there's little separation between miner and the Savage's glistening silver ore. The level could have been as deep as 1,300 feet below the surface. And the blur to the right hides evidence of a second miner, poised to hammer the drill held by his partner.

and noses and dressed in gay colored clothes." They were a touchy, easily offended lot. They did not like whistling or being watched. If miners neglected to leave them crumpets and pasties, Knockers blew out their candles, hid tools, stole pipes and tobacco, and dropped rocks on their heads. But if treated kindly and as friends, Knockers pointed the way to Sun Mountain's silver treasure.

Non-Cornish miners warmed to the notion of Tommyknockers, long convinced that spirits—"the ethereal bodies of departed miners"—haunted their workplaces.

As for rats—the Comstock was alive with rats—and they too were the Honest Miner's friend. He never killed them or shooed them off, and they therefore became "quite tame and saucy." They lived well off scraps of a lunch's meat and bones, and kept the place from stinking up. As pets, they were "Jake" or "Bobby."

Dan De Quille, a close friend of Mark Twain, carrying on after his sudden departure.

Both rats and Knockers warned miners of an impending cave-in. Agitated, rats would scamper about as if possessed; Knockers, in echoing, sepulchral voices, would bellow warnings.

With the Comstock's ore unstable and friable, cave-ins were inevitable, and if a man happened to be in the wrong place at the wrong time, fatal. As described by Dan De Quille:

> A man who has worked in the mines for years will walk into a chute in a musing mood, or run an ore car into the main shaft and be pulled in after it. Scores of blasting accidents might be mentioned—accidents that occurred from premature explosions; by persons coming upon blasts at the moment of their explosion.[16]

De Quille's list of hazards rambles on. Of Virginia's many thousands of miners, one in twenty were seriously injured, and one in eighty killed.

Timothy O'Sullivan would have been mightily relieved to take leave of this miasma, to breathe deeply the cold winter air. His was a landmark achievement—to be ignored. His underground images would be cut from the 40th Parallel Expedition's official report, representing as they did a dark, claustrophobic side of nineteenth-century industrial progress. Unlettered men battering rock, day-in, day-out.

Better to celebrate the vast, inviting scenic West.

———•◆•———

WITH A BACKGROUND OF SNOW shrouding the Savage's surface workings, O'Sullivan was asked to photograph a "safety cage" with

16 *The Big Bonanza*, 145, with descriptions of accidents continuing to 148.

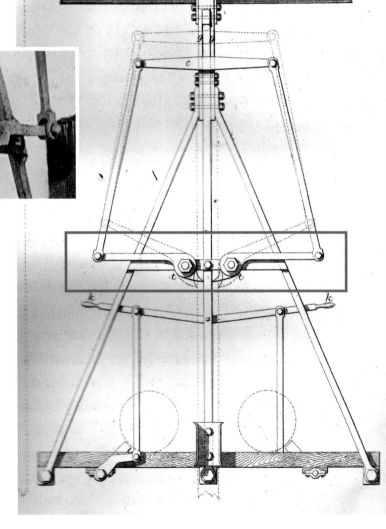

Plate VII.

Scale : $\frac{1}{20}$.

Fig. 2.

a new, life-saving feature. But what's that on its far side? A man's pair of legs, but what has happened to the rest of him?

He's there all right—but holding a white card so the viewer can clearly see two spring-loaded "dogs," as shown in a close-up detail and the cage's schematic.

As the cage was hoisted up or dropped down a shaft, it would be guided by two wooden rails flanked by stout iron "dogs"—that were held open by the weight of the cage and the pull of its cable. If all was well, they'd remain open, but should the cable snap and lose its tension, the dogs would bite the guide rails—and thwart a plunge to oblivion.

While O'Sullivan was in Virginia, this happened, with miners in the stalled cage not the least bit the worse for wear. Indeed, they were puzzled as to what exactly was wrong. Regrettably, there was nothing to prevent a parted cable from recoiling up a shaft and wreaking havoc in a hoist house, with men there lucky to escape the fury of a great, writhing steel snake. Dan De Quille, now the *Enterprise's* designated mining reporter, elaborated that the cable

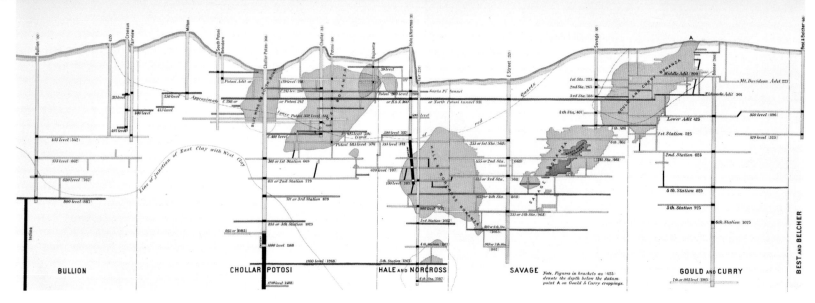

A cross-section of central Comstock mines and their bonanzas.

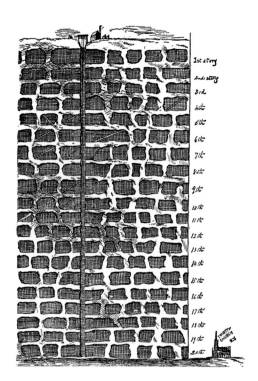

A popular illustration of the Comstock—deep and treacherously honeycombed. With Wall Street's 280 foot Trinity Church for scale.

would "cut a broad road through the whole length of the ceiling, taking off large joists and beams as though they were so many bars of soap, and killing or wounding all who may be in the way of the flying fragments."

De Quille was to sigh, "in short, there is no safety either above or below ground."

———————◆———————

THOUGH LOATHE to illustrate the grittiness of how silver was actually mined, the 40th Parallel expedition's report included a number of cross-sections of the distribution of silver ore along the Comstock lode. And these gave rise to a geological debate: Was or was not the Comstock a "true fissure vein" welling up from the depths of the earth? If so, there was the dizzying prospect of a "bottom that can never be reached by man, and its great wealth can never be exhausted."[17] The deeper, the richer! Maybe so, maybe

17   Grant H. Smith, *The History of the Comstock Lode* (Reno, NV: Nevada Bureau of Mines and Geology, 1943), 32.

not. What was *certain* was that the Comstock's ore occurred in great lumps dubbed "bonanzas."

And a daunting question arose, puzzling mine owners and miners alike: how could a bonanza's treasure be extracted without the roof and walls of a resulting cavern (called a "stope") disastrously collapsing? Wrecking a mine; snuffing miners.

Mine superintendents puzzled this without success. But then, a San Francisco director of the Ophir operation got wind of a young, émigré German engineer who might offer a solution.

The director posed the question: "What would you do if you had a quartz lode fifty or sixty feet wide?"

Philip Deidesheimer replied that he had never heard of such a thing, then quietly added, "I would like to study the place."

Ordered the agitated director, "Go to Virginia City tomorrow at my expense!"

Three weeks and Philip Deidesheimer had a solution, a scheme he called "square sets." Each set would be a box of 12-inch-square posts, 6 feet high and 5 feet long. The upper ends of these posts would be precisely notched to fit one to another, and create additional "sets" that could be expanded up, sideways, and even down, enabling the mining of a stope from wall to wall. If there was a danger of instability, upward flights of sets could be packed with waste rubble.

———— ·•◦•· ————

Virginia City wasn't all there was to the Comstock Lode. Some four and a half miles in length, it trended west under a ridge— the "Divide"—to beneath a sister settlement of Gold Hill. There, miners, rooting about, had encountered a hive of bees atop a deposit of silver, more and more silver. Thus the Yellow-Jacket

The Diedesheimers, an elegant and soon-to-be-very-rich couple.

Square sets replaced the silver one, no matter its mass, no matter its course. A mine owner's dream.

Diedesheimer's simple, sturdy concept.

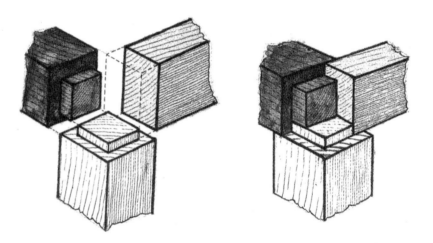

How his prefabricated posts were fitted. No nails were required; the earth's weight and pressure held everything in place.

Gold Hill from the west, with Virginia City over the ridge to the left.

Mine, and to the south, the adjoining Crown Point and Belcher, all tapping bonanzas.

Lining the steep canyon down to Devil's Gate, Gold Hill was a noisy, industrial hodge-podge, with a serene exception on up a side canyon. It was there that an early-day Johntown boarding house keeper and washerwoman—Eilley Orrem—accepted a small claim from a miner who couldn't pay his bill. A few nights later, washing dishes, she mentioned this to a soft-spoken fellow in whom she'd taken an interest, Lemuel "Sandy" Bowers. He blinked. "Really?" For it turned out that he had come into the possession of an adjoining claim.

Gold Hill mines reflecting their owners' hankering for prestige.

Bowers Canyon, Gold Hill.

Once a placer miner, once a washerwoman: Sandy & Eilley.

The scene of the Bowers' banquet, a second incarnation of the city's International Hotel.

One thing led to another, and the pair were hitched, partners in matrimony, mining—and blessed fortune.

Fortune there was! Their combined claim, just twenty feet wide, holed into a sizeable bonanza. And here was proof that common folks, as well as San Francisco speculators and eastern syndicates, could strike it rich—and make the most of it, with Eilley and Sandy now planning an imposing mansion on the shore of Washoe Lake on down in the Carson Valley, and furnishing it with the best to be had on distant shores.

The pair hired the International Hotel and invited near all of Virginia City to a farewell banquet. Sandy's speech was quoted in the *Enterprise*:

I've had powerful good luck in this country, an' now I've got money to throw at the birds. There aren't no chance for a gentleman to spend his coin in this country, an' so me and Mrs. Bowers is goin' ter Yoorup to take in the sights.

Sandy concluded:

Now me and Mrs. Bowers is going to see the Queen of England and other great men of them countries, and I hope ye'll all join in a drink to Mrs. Bower's health. There's plenty of champagne, and money ain't no object.

———•◦•———

THE BOWERS FORTHWITH embarked on an epic Grand Tour, with ample funds to be thrown to the birds. In London, checking into a ritzy hotel, they rang for a clerk, to request that he draw up a bill of sale for their suite's large walnut bed, a bureau festooned with walnut grapes, and a similarly decorated night potty, adding instructions to ship the lot to their Lake Washoe mansion, now abuilding.

In due course, they rang the bell of the American Embassy, where they bent the ear of Ambassador Charles Francis Adams, a Boston blueblood. Eilley explained that, though she was hazy as to how, she was related to Queen Victoria. Could Adams arrange a tea? Not knowing what to make of these far West rustics, Adams explained that was not possible, as the queen was currently residing at her Balmoral Castle in Scotland.

Well then, decided Eilley, it would be off to the Highlands—the land of her birth—where, as she pressed local gentry, the prospects of an audience took a discouraging turn. Her Majesty, she was told, received no divorced ladies. Which put Eilley out of the running, for on the road to Virginia City and her betrothal to Sandy, she had acquired and discarded two Mormon husbands.

Too bad about that, but in any case, the Bowers were off to the City of Lights, with the hope of attending a ball given by Napoleon and the Empress Eugenie—a cousin, Eilley believed. With an invite failing to materialize, the pair opted for a round of Christmas shopping, parting with $20,000 in a single day. On the Rue de Richelieu, Eilley dropped by the shop of the fashionable Monsieur Gagalin, there to select the look that best suited her.

Sandy watched as his wife was draped with Ottoman velour, China rose silk, black velvet—textiles ameliorating her royal snubs. Himself, he favored elaborately-carved antiques and handsome morocco-bound books, though he'd yet to learn to read.

From silver candlesticks to silver stairway railing, they accumulated furnishings for their mansion. And continuing their siege of the crowned heads of Europe, they were told an invitation was on its

Eilley in a similar
gown, fitted for
her presentation.

Her Majesty.

Was Eilley a Favori? A Penelope? A Preiur?

Sandy was partial to pianos. When queried if he'd like to order up sheet music, he replied, "I'll take one of each."

way to the coronation of Italy's Victor Emmanuel. Though it failed to materialize, no matter, after an eleven-month toot their Washoe Lake mansion was finished, landscaped with palms and goldfish ponds, and awaited their return.

Their enjoyment of the good life, sadly, was fleeting, for their Gold Hill mine's rich vein of silver had pinched down—and out, and with it, their once-staggering income. Desperate to right the situation, Sandy decamped the mansion and bunked up the hill, with little to show for his efforts. His health took a turn for the worse. He came down with a cough that drinks at the Miner's Exchange saloon couldn't slake, and he died on April 21, 1868, the dust of the Bowers mine clogging his lungs.

Eilley was widowed, poverty stricken. But, if she could help it, this would not be a case of rags–to–riches and then back-to-rags.

She had long had a gift, a penchant for "second sight." Either squinting through a Scottish "peep stone" or gazing a crystal ball, she could determine the whereabouts of items lost or stolen, predict mining success or disaster, even glimpse Virginia City's future.

The Bowers' dream.

And she'd communicate with Sandy; he'd advise her from wherever he'd gone.

She'd become *The Seeress of Washoe*.

67

DREAMERS *and* SCHEMERS

THE YOUNG AND THE OLD, individuals of high or low estate, were sooner or later up the stairs of the Sutterley Brothers' C Street studio, there to pose in front of a Greek temple and a sylvan landscape.[18] Few had come to Virginia City against their will (Chinese prostitutes, collared desperados); the vast majority "arrived with all kinds of air castles packed in their carpetbag."[19] They cherished a dream—and had a scheme to achieve it.

Dream and scheme, the two words are not, as they might seem, incompatible; together, they connote a hope and a plan. And up in this remote corner of Nevada there was an undeniable excitement in the fact that millions of millions of dollars worth of silver lay under your feet, begging you, cajoling you, to claim your share.

There were differing rewards, sought and achieved. In the gallery on the facing page, Amy Stone turned heads as "the French Vivandiere." Father Manogue, six foot three inches tall and weighing in at 300 pounds, was declared "A great man in every sense of the word." First Ward policemen Benjamin Ballou, sadly, would be cut short in his efforts to maintain law and order, shot and killed while arresting a drunk in 1866.

And the day came when a stout cigar salesman from San Francisco was to become a much admired champion of what "a man with sand"—gumption and drive—could achieve. An admirer wrote that

18 Whereas Sutterley's studio, along with its contents (and the better part of Virginia City) was consumed in an 1875 fire, the opposite images were preserved in the personal collection of Gold Hill journalist and volunteer firefighter Alf Doten (his portrait on page 70).

19 Actress Lotta Crabtree, quoted in David Dempsey, *The Triumphs and Trials of Lotta Crabtree* (New York: William Morrow & Co., 1968).

Policeman Benjamin Ballou.

Ingénue Amy Stone.

Clement Sutterley, photographer.

Reverend Father Patrick Manogue.

Saloon keeper Tom Peasley.

Virginia's citizens, each with a hope—be it of sailing home to China, heroism, gaining respect for one's people, or keeping the peace.

Marie, Susie & Nellie.

Volunteer fireman Alf Doten.

Young Winnemucca.

District Judge William Haydon.

"He does not seem to know the definition of but two phrases in the English language. They are "I can't" and "you shant." His mottoes seem to be "Go ahead," and "Nothing shall stop me." [20]

His signature flowing whiskers testified to his doughtiness; they concealed an ear to mouth slash inflicted by a stockbroker he'd denounced as a scoundrel.

A German-Jewish émigré, Adolph Sutro believed he could offer a solution to a growing threat in the Comstock's deep mines. They had been plagued by crumbling rock (at least it was silver), near-unbearable heat—and now water. Jets of it—at temperatures of as

high as 160 degrees!—springing, then gushing from the strike of a miner's pick, and flooding lower levels with thousands, nay millions, of gallons of water. Pumps ran round the clock, but barely diminished a spreading, subterranean sea.

Sutro proposed that the mines be drained by a 20,500 foot inclined tunnel driven from the foot of Sun Mountain. At a depth of 1,640 feet, it would intercept the Savage shaft, which in turn offered a connection to near every major Comstock mine. It was a daunting, ingenious scheme, and he'd be the man to pull it off. He had studied the technology of mining, and on a grass-roots level fancied himself one with the Comstock's miners. Accordingly, he had his picture taken.

20 Mary McNair Matthews, *Ten Years in Nevada* (Buffalo, NY: James Baker, 1880) 200.

70

Sutro the humble miner. Pay no attention to the fact that the mine is a studio set, with his patent dress shoes a giveaway.

The tunnel, with branches to major mines.
Note the platted town of Sutro—to possibly
eclipse Virginia City.

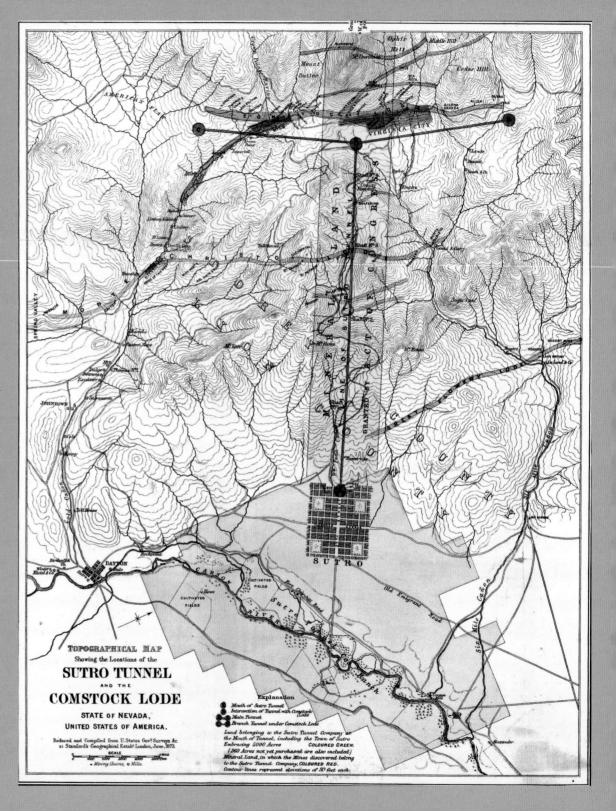

TOPOGRAPHICAL MAP
Showing the Locations of the
SUTRO TUNNEL
AND THE
COMSTOCK LODE
STATE OF NEVADA,
UNITED STATES OF AMERICA.

Reduced and Compiled from U. States Gov.t Surveys &c.
at Stanford's Geographical Establ.t London, June, 1873.

SCALE

Mining Claims, o Mills.

Explanation
Mouth of Sutro Tunnel
Intersection of Tunnel with Comstock Lode
Main Tunnel
Branch Tunnel under Comstock Lode
Land belonging to the Sutro Tunnel Company at
the Mouth of Tunnel, including the Town of Sutro
Embracing 5000 Acres   COLOURED GREEN.
(360 Acres not yet purchased are also included.)
Mineral Land, in which the Mines discovered belong
to the Sutro Tunnel Company, COLOURED RED.
Contour lines represent elevations of 50 feet each.

Variations of the man-with-the-pickaxe image would adorn Sutro promotional pamphlets, progress reports, and stock offerings. He projected his tunnel's cost to be in the neighborhood of $5 million.

The Comstock's miners were all for the idea; in the event of a cave-in or fire, the tunnel would offer a ready-made escape route. Mine owners met, gave the project a nod, and agreed to underwrite a substantial share of its cost.

But then Adolph got a little carried away with himself. Not only would mines be drained, he announced, but the tunnel would serve as a haulage way for the Comstock's ore. That is, for a modest fee per ton. At this, the mine owner's balked. Only to have Sutro further proclaim that miners could come and go through the tunnel, and comfortably dwell in a new town platted at its mouth. Modestly named "Sutro," it would be well down the mountain from wind-racked Virginia City—and render it a ghost town, where "owls would roost."

With the prospect of buildings worth less than the nails holding them together, that didn't set well with anyone. Not at all. Promised support was withdrawn, from mine owners and miners alike. In the ornate prose of the day,

> The tunnel scheme was blossoming rarely and the fruit was all but plucked in anticipation, when a sudden frost blighted the opening buds. The announcement [of the mine owners] was a bitter disappointment to Mr. Sutro. He had worked with tireless energy and was just raising the cup of fruition to his lips, when it was dashed to the ground.[21]

Not only was Sutro out in the cold, he was actively shunned. In

21 *Comstock Mines and Miners*, 236–7.

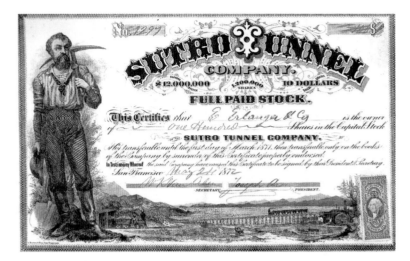

Sutro referred to his likeness as "The Honest Miner."

his words, he was treated as if he were "an absconding bank clerk, a forger, criminal," with blame due not so much to Comstockers, but to the devious manipulations of San Francisco's Bank of California and its driving force, William C. Ralston.

And to execute Ralston's orders and further his schemes, one William Sharon was to become "Virginia's Iago."

Fully realizing that the money flooding the Pacific Coast had its origin in the Comstock, Ralston had dispatched Sharon to open a Virginia City branch, and together the pair set their sights on creating "a fortified monopoly." Sooner or later, they and their "Bank Ring" would buy out mine owners, mill operators, timber cutters—everyone. Or if need be, mercilessly drive them out of business.

But first, they set their sights on Adolph Sutro, who innocently believed them to be a banking resource. As if he hadn't sufficiently damaged his cause with his grandiose statements, the Bank of California forthwith persuaded Virginia's mine owners to not only abandon their backing, but to join in signing a one-sentence telegram to Nevada's senators, lest Congress entertain the idea of

W. C. Ralston and
William Sharon.
Imperious and
cold-blooded.

government funding. "WE ARE OPPOSED TO THE SUTRO TUNNEL
PROJECT AND DESIRE IT DEFEATED IF POSSIBLE."

With the realization that his banking friends were now his en-
emies, with mine owners their lackeys, Sutro was to recall:

> Nearly all the persons who had stood by me now deserted
> me as if I had an infectious disease. Every miserable cur and
> hirelings of that bank turned the cold shoulder on me. But
> the ring had got hold of the wrong man. I was not so easily
> to be disposed of.

He wasn't. He would tirelessly promote and sell stock. He'd tap
sources in England and on the Continent, with foreign banks eager
for a share of American enterprise.

———————

W. C. RALSTON AND WILLIAM SHARON conspired: how to dispose
of resolute, stubborn Adolph Sutro. They considered his promise to
move the Comstock's ore and had to admit, the idea made sense.
Gravity would be on Sutro's side. The ore could be dropped down
to the Comstock's 1,640 foot level, then rolled down the tunnel's
gently sloping incline to mills on the Carson River. This was certainly better than the current state of affairs, with close to 3,000
prairie schooners hitched to 15,000 animals hauling ore downhill
from Virginia and out through Devil's Gate.

It came to them: build a railroad! Take the wind out of the sails
of "that damned old Assyrian carpetbagger"!

Sharon quietly made the rounds of the officials of the counties
through which the railroad would pass, and telegraphed Ralston of
their donation of $500,000 "for the common good." The funds had
initially been earmarked for Sutro's tunnel, as had an additional

A Currier & Ives lithograph titled "Lightning Express." It is a classic Baldwin American with a 4-4-0 configuration (in railroad talk, four guide wheels behind the cowcatcher, four large drivers, and no trailing wheels). Virginia would have its own "Lightning Express" to Carson City, and then on to a mainline connection to San Francisco.

$700,000 now pried from Virginia's mine owners. Sharon then summoned the best mining surveyor on the Comstock, Superintendent James of the Sierra Nevada Company. He got right to the point.

"James, can you run a railroad from Virginia City to the Carson River?"

"Yes."

"Do it at once."

Sharon ordered rolling stock and engines: *Moguls* from San Francisco's Union Iron Works, as well as *Americans* from Philadephia's Baldwin Locomotive Works. They'd be suited to the task; they were compact and sturdy. Moreover, they'd appeal to Virginia's penchant for the flamboyant in that they'd be festooned with brass scrollwork and bedecked with flags. In railroad history, they'd be celebrated as machines with spunk, and sand—personality!—superior to

Initially dragged to Carson City from the mainline at Reno by 14-yoke ox teams.

anything before or since. And no matter their questionable recruitment on the Comstock, they'd be the pride of its working men and women, and the delight of its little kids.

In February of 1869, a base of operations was set up in Carson City—offices, yards, shops, and a roundhouse. Grading began, and by April, 1,200 men, most all Chinese, were working out of thirty-eight camps. In the rugged country approaching Virginia, they dug tunnels nearly 600 feet in length, and constructed a spectacular 500-foot trestle.

They'd soon be laying track, on its way around Cape Horn from England.

———

WHILE IN VIRGINIA, Adolph Sutro lived alone, cooked for himself, and was forever burning his rice pot. And he couldn't help but be discouraged. If the game here was a chess match, black was sweeping his board, with mine owners pawns of Ralston, Sharon, and their Bank Ring. He was all but checkmated by their railroad. As well, there was a hitch to his tunnel's promise to drain the Comstock's mines: a number of shafts had encountered a deeper, drier geologic zone. In addition, massive Cornish pumps—similar to those in British tin mines—were coming into play.

Until seven in the morning of Wednesday, April 7, 1869.

In the Yellow-Jacket mine, a departing graveyard shift had apparently left a candle stuck to a timber—and burning.

Day shifters, lowered to the 800-foot level, smelled smoke, and before they could escape, were trapped by advancing, searing sheets of flames. The mine's steam whistle shrieked. Gold Hill and Virginia fire teams were on their way, to face smoke billowing up from the shaft—so dense there was little they could do. At nine o'clock, they were able to descend and recover two bodies, and four more at noon.

The Yellow-Jacket headframe and, in the distance, the Crown Point mine.

By then, the fire has spread to the adjacent Crown Point mine, where men, barely alive, were hoisted in a cage, only to collapse and be crushed between the cage and its shaft's timbers.

An empty cage was lowered to the thousand-foot level. On it, a lantern lit a pasteboard scrawled with:

> We are fast subduing the fire. It is death to attempt to come up from where you are. We shall get you out soon. The gas in the shaft is terrible, and produces sure and speedy death. Write a word to us and send it up on the cage, and let us know where you are.

No answer. All were dead.

The *Territorial Enterprise*'s Dan De Quille was there, to write:

> The wives, children, and relatives of the lost flocked as near to the mouths of the shafts [of now, several mines] as they were allowed to come, their grief and lamentations causing tears to course down the cheeks of the most stout-hearted. "Lost! Lost! Lost!" was the despairing cry uttered by the women whose husbands were below. As a cage rose up, there was a wail from the women, who could with difficulty be restrained from climbing over the ropes stretched to keep back the crowd. "Oh God! Who is it this time?"

Forty-five miners were killed.

When miners and firemen were able to enter the Yellow-Jacket and Crown Point mines, hot water boiled under their feet; they choked on steam and sulfur fumes. A hell on earth. Though sealed off, the fire burned on; three years later rocks on the 800-foot level were red hot.

ADOLPH SUTRO WAS BOTH heartbroken and furious. This was precisely the disaster his tunnel could prevent in providing a down-and-then-out escape route for trapped miners.

He rented Virginia's opera house, called a meeting. The Comstock's miners packed it to the rafters.

Sutro strode onto the stage, to ask:

> Will the people of Nevada see me crushed out now? Will you not see fair play when one man has the pluck to stand up against the crowd? I shall tell the truth, without fear or reservation, for I have come here to "fight it out on this line," and I intend to do this "though the heavens fall."

In no uncertain terms, he denounced the avarice of Ralston, Sharon, and the Bank of California, "vampires that nearly suck you dry." What did they care for the common man? In brief, hard-hitting sentences, he contrasted the selfishness of these capitalists with the access and safety his tunnel would afford.

For the Bank Ring, "the first pick struck into the tunnel will be the first pick into their graves."

The crowd cheered; the Miner's Union promptly raised $50,000 by subscription, and invested it in Sutro Tunnel Company stock.

Sutro broke ground. He hired miners, sunk ventilation shafts, and ordered specially designed cars towed by either hand-pumpers or mules.

A MONTH AFTER Adolph Sutro commenced his tunnel, the Bank Ring's Chinese crews had laid a requisite twenty-one miles of rails, and the engine Lyon puffed up the grade to Gold Hill, to be hailed

His German accent aside, his bitter eloquence would mesmerize his audience.

The man in the black hat and coat is almost certainly Father Manogue, hapless in his effort to comfort a bereft crowd. In the background, smoke billowed from the Yellow-Jacket mine.

There was some question as to what to name the line, with an early suggestion the "Virginia, Carson, & Truckee River"—the VC&TR—which was promptly nicknamed the "Very Crooked & Terribly Rough" railroad, or better yet, "Sharon's Crooked Railroad." Sharon and his associates settled on the V&T, the "Virginia & Truckee." The engine is a 2-6-0 Mogul.

The engine plate and throttle of still-surviving engine no. 22, the Inyo.

The Sutro tunnel's rapidly advanced pilot drift (and ventilation pipe) ran to the right. It would subsequently be widened to accommodate a second track to ferry miners in, and cart rock out.

Set to the left in the above image, a theodolite *(right)* insured that the tunnel would accurately intersect the Comstock.

by a din of mine whistles and a cheering crowd. With drinks on the Bank of California, the *Enterprise* declared that "nature is everywhere better when palpitating engines snort steam across her acres, plunging madly onward."

Present at the festivities, William Sharon couldn't help but be pleased. His personal cut of the construction costs had been $2,000 a day, with more to come.

As he was later to boast, "I built that road without it costing me a dollar." So much for Adolph Sutro and his misbegotten dream. The

line would presently be hauling 20,000 tons of ore a month. And the Bank Ring would be free to continue its "plundering without the slightest sense of shame, or shadow of remorse." [22]

———•◦•———

Would Adolph Sutro *now* forsake his dream? Not a chance. Down the mountain from Virginia, he built himself a mansion, and

22 Warren B. Ewer, *Mining & Scientific Press*, January 18, 1873.

with renewed energy pushed his tunnel ever deeper into the heart of Sun Mountain. He'd been thwarted, but he was damned if he'd throw in the towel.

Visitors to Sutro's mansion were welcomed not by a bitter curmudgeon (as one might expect), but by a gracious and good-humored host. Before a well-laid dinner, he'd ask guests to share a story or perform a trick, a magic trick. He'd get things going by shuffling across a carpet—building up a static electric charge—and then, turning on a gas jet, ignite it with a snap of his fingers.

A metaphor for what he aimed to accomplish? Make no mistake, he had told the crowd at the opera house,

My fellow honest miners, I made a sacred vow that I would carry out this work if I had to devote the remainder of my life to it, and would defend my rights as long as the breath of life was in me.

A stereoscopic view of Sutro's mansion. It overlooked his tunnel's portal.

In a rare moment of relaxation.

85

AMUSEMENTS

IT'S 7 A.M. IN THE CRYSTAL SALOON. A number of miners having stopped by for a tad of "spirituous fortification," their morning shifts were now dropping into the depths of the earth, and there was now a lull in the establishment's round-the-clock hours. The Crystal fancied itself the top of the line, the most luxurious, "the millionaire's saloon." Be that it may, now was the time to slosh its spit-splattered floor with buckets of water, and empty its strategically placed, but oft ignored, cuspidors.

Customers were few—merchants on their way to open their shops, the odd parched policeman—and even odder, a wooly fellow, a sheep.

It will go every morning to the nearest saloon, put its fore paws upon the bar, and bleat for his morning dram. After he is waited upon he will go out the door, look up and down the sidewalk until he sees an old friend coming. He will follow him about until he gives him a chew of tobacco. He'll then hie off to his stable and nap. He is a fine, fat, fellow, and quite intelligent-looking.[23]

Things would pick up come lunchtime—with a light repast often offered free with drinks. And then, in anticipation of steam whistles signaling the 3 p.m. end of the morning shift, the Crystal's bartenders multiplied in numbers, busily washing and drying glasses and stacking them in back-bar pyramids. As to their calling, Mark Twain had noted that

23 *Ten Years in Nevada*, 242.

A century and a quarter ago, a morning lull in
the Crystal Saloon.

A surviving chandelier imported from Paris.

"the cheapest and easiest way to become an influential man and be looked up to by the community was to stand behind a bar, wear a cluster-diamond pin, and sell whisky. I am not sure but that the saloon-keeper had a shade higher rank than any other member of society. His opinion had weight." [24]

Off-shift miners were soon on their way, but not before shedding their grubby digging togs, showering, and donning vests, jackets, and brushed felt hats. They combed their hair in changing room mirrors. "If you're going to drink," said one, "drink dressed up."

They had their pride, were good as anyone, including their boss mine owners, with whom they might well rub shoulders.

The Crystal was soon a lively hubbub of imprecations, shouts, and colorfully told stories, expressed in language featuring a "broadly humorous or quaintly burlesque use of words, for here is Shakespeare's English." The Bard was wildly popular in Virginia City, and accordingly, a man might refer to another as a "Hamlet"— or an "Iago."

Indeed, there was a theatrical element to daily life here—a western incarnation of both the light-heartedness and drama of the Old Globe.

24   Mark Twain, *Roughing It* (New York: Harper & Bros., 1913) 254.

They'd soon be dispensing their share of a Virginia's annual "75,000 gallons of liquor, chiefly whisky, exclusive of beer and wine." (As noted by an historian at the time, Eliot Lord.)

A respectably dressed crowd. Is there a Polonius and Hamlet at the bar? And a Falstaff?

An approximation of two blocks of C Street, with a cluster of "two-bit" saloons across the way, and "one-bit" saloons in the foreground.
The coins in the illustration are Comstock silver, struck at Nevada's Carson City mint.

The Crystal modestly billed itself as "surpassing in luxury and in the perfection of its appointments any gentlemen's club in Western America." Situated on the west side of C Street, it was a leading "two-bit" (25 cent) establishment, for that was the charge for a drink.

Rowdier, less literate "one-bit" bars were across the street, on the east side.

"One bit" customers tended to be on the rougher side and not so courtly of speech. A teamster would hold forth and, "O Plutus! Such swearing—a sliding scale of oaths to which swearing in all other parts of the world is as the murmuring of a gentle brook to the volume and rush and thunder of a cataract."[25] Or, without warning, a bozo would reel through the door bellowing "I'm a war horse from the hills and a fighter from hell!" And there'd be, no surprise, an ensuing "shebang" punctuated by "a smashing of glass, a crashing of chairs, bottles and tumblers, fierce yells, bitter curses, and in short a fearful commotion." It was said of such a fellow, "When he had a frolic, he wanted to see things whiz!"[26]

25 The ever-colorful J. Ross Browne, on a return trip to Virginia described in *Washoe Revisited* (Oakland, CA: Biobooks, 1957) 37.
26 Dan De Quille, *The Big Bonanza*, 276, 278.

One-bit bought a man a drink at
the Antler Saloon.

The Antler Saloon was "no nursery for tender consciences."

"Every fourth door was a saloon of one or the other kind, with great displays of elks' and bears' heads," or in this case a boar's. (Mary McNair Mathews, *Ten Years in Nevada*)

Lore had it that early faro cards were printed with a tiger on their backs. The game, then, invited sports to "Buck the Tiger" (as on the broadside at the beginning of this chapter). Though no such cards are known to still exist, here at least, the tiger bares his fangs.

Steps away, faro players would enjoy, even applaud the spectacle, then resume their game. It was by far the most popular gambling game in the American West. A tenderfoot could grasp its essentials in but a few minutes, and it was fast, intense—and invariably duplicitous, with many a means for the house to cheat: sanded or trimmed cards, holdouts, a spring-loaded dealing box, to name a few. An accomplished sharp could perform a "faro shuffle" that would advantageously pair up as many as eight cards, and up his advantage from a modest 2 percent to a lucrative 25 percent.

Beware the manipulations of the likes of dealer Kettle Belly Brown, backslapping and crooked!

Yet while faro was to undo—and ruin—sports in a host of western camps, that was less the case in Virginia. For here, there was another, more profitable way to place your bets, or so you might have thought.

Mining stocks!

Up and down C Street, they were peddled by caterwauling, curbstone brokers. On portable boards, they chalked up the rise and fall of sales, both in Virginia and off in San Francisco. Differing stocks were avidly debated. They had their virtues, their liabilities. Which to choose?

Circulating the crowd, professional speculators would weigh in, but who could trust "the man who worked claims with his jaw instead of his pick?" Down alleyways, men huddled in corners consulting in low tones, whispering "confidential" information on what the boys in the depths of a given mine were on to. Describing a "con" man, Mary McNair Matthews wrote,

> I did not exactly like the tone of his voice, or his looks either, for he did not look smart, not even enough to be a rogue, although he talked through his nose, and was very soft-spoken—one of the best signs of a rogue I ever noticed. I know two brokers in Virginia City who have this peculiar way of speaking, and I think either of them would rob his mother of her last dime.[27]

There was a term for all this: "stock devilment." Nevertheless, each stock had its story, its appeal— or not.

27 *Ten Years in Nevada*, 102.

Enhancing an illusion of fair play, a "case counter" enabled a sport to keep track of his game.

A homemade dealing box. Note the absence of numbers on the cards, challenging a befuddled player to distinguish, say, an eight from a nine.

Speculation consumes a C Street throng, "gathered as thick as bees on clover," their focus a stock bulletin board. The fellow to the right apparently has had quite enough of this.

Ever tantalizing were the tales of overnight fortunes. The Crown Point, devastated by fire and shunned by investors, had its stock drop to $3 a share. But then, they'd struck it rich at the 1,100 foot level—and the stock? Now going for $1,825 a share.

Surveying C Street, San Francisco's *Mining Review* concluded:

The market extends everywhere; the buyers and sellers of stock include the millionaire and the mendicant, the modest matron and the brazen courtesan, the prudent man of business and the gambler, the maidservant and her mistress, the banker and his customer.

And not to be forgotten in the daily excitement: the Comstock's dozen oyster vendors, on hand to feed the souls that fed the frenzy. Who knew when and where there'd be a next, underground excitement?

The first of the Comstock's bonanzas. Was the mine ripe for another?

A speculator's sample was rich, but was this a case of "bucking and bearing thereof"? (Using the sample as bait for a swindle.)

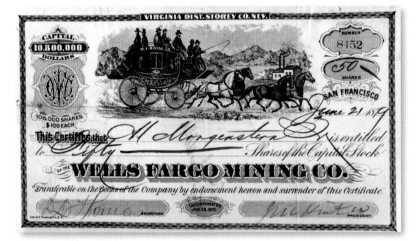

A nice design (by black artist Grafton T. Brown), but Wells Fargo might be off sticking with staging.

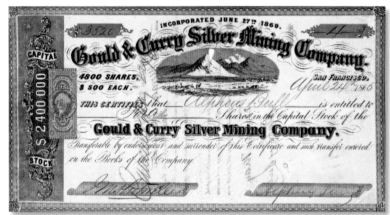

A sleeper? At a depth of 600 feet, the G & C's ore had bottomed out. But then, a recent cave-in could bode for the better. Rumor was that it laid bare a new deposit.

It was said that on C Street a man couldn't throw a stone at a dog "without first looking to see if contained a sulphuret or chloride" of silver.

The sun set earlier in Virginia than elsewhere in the West, slipping away behind the dusky, often snow-capped Sierra Nevada. The stock-obsessed crowd would disperse and head home, be it to a tidy cottage or a ramshackle boarding house. Or if fortune had smiled that afternoon, there'd be the option of a fancy restaurant.

The Comstock boasted a number. The French Rotisserie, the dining room in the International Hotel, Delmonico's. Then it would be time to spritz a little cologne, dust a frock coat, cinch a taffeta gown, dab a splash of perfume, and be off to the theater.

There were choices. At one point, five Shakespearean companies held forth, with appreciative audiences joining actors in the recitation of familiar soliloquys. At the same time, six other troupes presented vaudeville, a dog and pony act, and a musical version of

Looking downhill to D Street—and Maguire's Opera House, its name on the building's shadow side.

Uncle Tom's Cabin. On a lighter side, there was the "Best in Ethiopian entertainment" with the audience invited to join refrains of the catchy ditty:

Behind the hen house on my knees.
I think I hear a chicken sneeze,
Turkeys playing cards on the pumpkin vine,
Goose chaw tobacco, ducks drink wine.

Many venues were a step up from early-day hurdy-gurdy houses. The grandest was the Opera House operated by Thomas Maguire, a San Francisco impresario who fancied himself "the Napoleon of the stage."

Maguire's was richly carpeted—no sawdust on the floor here—and offered boxes furnished with gilt chairs and velvet railing. Glittering chandeliers hung from the ceiling; a magnificent curtain featured a Lake Tahoe sunset, "painted by a real artist from Italy." The house seated 1,600.

Befitting Virginia's polyglot population, Thomas Maguire's offerings were enthusiastically eclectic.

He staged prizefights as well as a battle between a bear and three bulldogs, and a then a bear and a bull, "but as the bull could not prod the bear into a fighting humor the audience left in disgust." There were brass band concerts, "Whoop-La" dancers, and "The Montgomery Queen's Great Show with the Only Female Somersault Rider in the World."

Rodolphus Hall, a "ventriloquist bugler," suffered nosebleeds due to the 8,000 foot altitude. He wrote his wife back in New Hampshire, "In fact everybody is affected the same way—it gives one a wild crazy feeling—and in truth there are, I think, more insane people in this country than any other."

Despite the theater's name, it is questionable if an opera was ever performed. That's not to say it didn't cater to the higher minded. Maguire courted Shakespeareans and they in turn enjoyed their stints here, plied with champagne and oysters and basking in applause, cheers, and rustic foot-stamping.

With a penchant for tragic roles, Helena Modjeska was America's leading Shakespearean actress. Marveled the *Enterprise*, "Why her acting just walks into a man's soul without knocking and takes possession of the whole ground floor." Junius Brutus Booth, Jr. (brother of John Wilkes) was both startled and pleased by the hisses and catcalls rained on his portrayal of Othello's Iago. And "the nation's darling," Lotta Crabtree, yet a child, played the banjo, danced the cat-choker, and was "extremely comic and half bashful." She was said to have sprinkled her red hair with cayenne pepper to make it sparkle in the theater's gaslights. She sang:

> I can play the banjo yes, indeed, I can
> I can play a tune upon the frying pan.
> I hollo like a steamboat 'fore she's gwine to stop;
> I can sweep a chimney and sing out at the top –
> Strike de toe and heel, cut de pigeon wing.
> Scratch gravel, slap de foot, dat's jus' de thing.

She was showered with silver and gold, collected by her mom, first in a shoe, then in a basket. Mama recalled, "The money came down on the stage like rain."

Dapper Thomas Maguire had a "chronic weakness for grandiose theater."

Helena Modjeska.

Little Lotta Crabtree.

Junius Brutus Booth, Jr.

The day came when posters heralded the arrival of a Miss Adah Isaacs Menken—and before she left, she'd be "The Menken" on the lips of every last Virginian. Her reputation preceded her. She had been captured by Texas Indians; she escaped; she wrote poetry; she willingly took risks, and did so lightly clad. A "shape artist," she was "the more undressed actress than any other on the American stage," traveling "with two immense cigar boxes full of clothing."

Impresario Maguire rubbed his hands. He'd redecorated his Opera House, had its ceiling painted with cupids and angels in "the gorgeous style of Louis XV." Virginians would now thrill as—

Miss ADAH Ascends and Descends to and from the Entire Height of this Immense Theater, lashed to the Bare-Back of the Wild Steed, a feat never accomplished by any other Lady in the World.

A Thrilling and Exciting Denouemont!

Loosely based on a poem penned by Lord Byron, the play was *Mazeppa!* The work of a hack dramatist, it was hardly great theater, but who on the Comstock cared? It was the end of Act I that mattered, combining as it did two pursuits dear to Miss Adah. The first was riding horses, the spirited the better.

The second pursuit—or rather, habit—was reclining, which she did at every possible opportunity, both on and off stage.

On her opening night, *she would simultaneously ride a horse and recline.* And do it essaying a man's role, the Tartar prince Ivan Mazeppa, who'd dared to love the daughter of a nasty Polish nobleman, who aimed to dispatch him (*her* in this case) to a certain death.

Maguire's Opera House was Standing Room Only.

The audience was rife with anticipation. In the past a dummy had been substituted for Act I's Death Ride, but not tonight. That was

ADAH ISAACS MENKEN—THE POET-ACTRESS. [With fac-simile of her hand writing.]

In Virginia, she'd be squired about by Sazerac Saloon keeper Tom Peasley (his portrait on page 70). She was said to delight in his panther-like tread—and in winning at his faro spread.

for lesser venues and lesser actresses. A patron whispered, "I hope the poor girl doesn't break her reckless neck."

The curtain rose on a castle courtyard. A crag soared upward and out of sight.

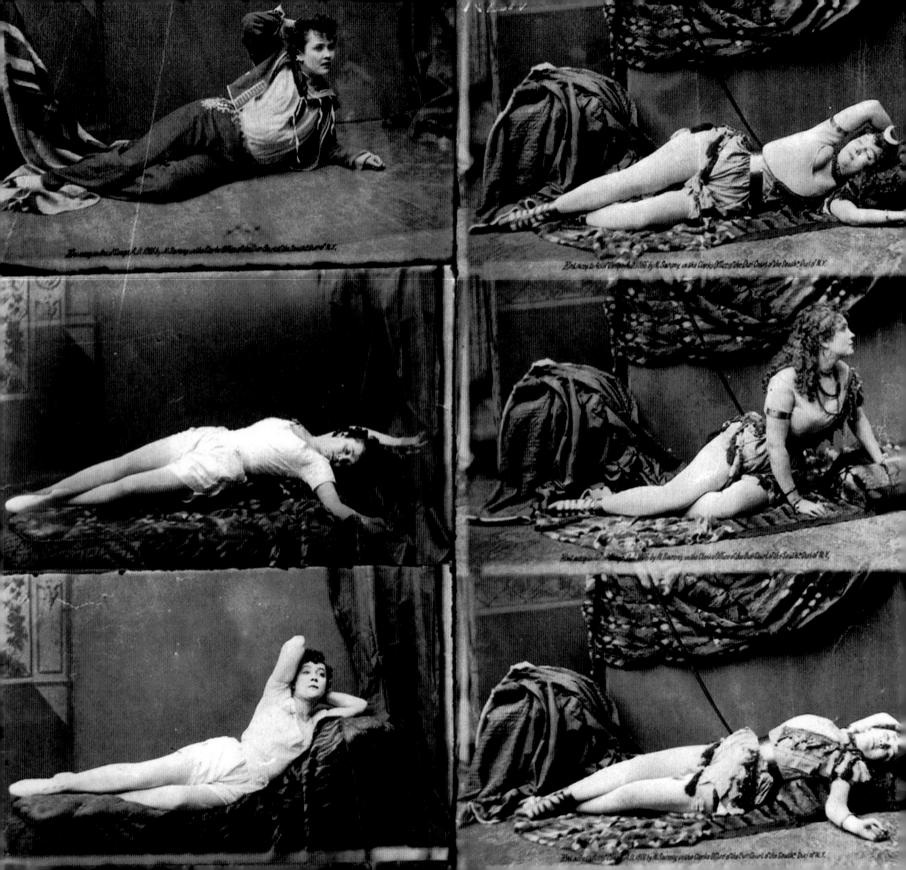

Actors strode on stage, declaimed, drifted off, then reappeared. Prince Ivan (Miss Adah) defied the Polish nobleman. The audience fidgeted. Where was the shape artist they'd been promised? She was costumed, elaborately so.

Half an hour in, the stage cleared and the gaslights dimmed. A horse bolted onstage, barely restrained by three men clinging to its bridle. Then on came The Menken, dragged by ruthless guards. The audience gasped! She was naked, or nearly so! It was hard to say, for now theatrical moonlight lit the scene, glistening her beautiful body, white as snow, as she was bound to the horse's back. A last cord was knotted; the guards sprang back. A drum rolled; the fiery black steed reared, wildly snorted, then galloped across the stage and onto a mountain trail coursing upward through jagged rocks, across a bridge over a roaring stream, and was lost to view high beyond the proscenium.

Men cheered. Women wept. The Ride of Death! The audience was on its feet, clapping and stamping. The curtain fell. Men in the boxes swore that she'd left any vestige of tights in her dressing room. Exclaimed one, "Stunning creature, by gad!" Thomas Maguire congratulated himself on his entrepreneurial cunning—and its appeal to Comstockers, themselves actors and actresses in the drama that was Virginia City.

The Menken reappeared, gracefully bowed. She'd survived Act I. At the end of the performance, there'd be bouquets of flowers, even watches, tossed onto the stage.

A fellow in the audience would, as an old timer, look back—with his proudest boast not the fact that he had looked the fierce Comanche in the eye or drank with old Jim Bridger, but that *"I'd seen Adah on that horse."*

Left: Whether a dramatic offering called for it or not, Miss Adah reclined.

A *Mazeppa!* poster. With Junius Brutus Booth, Jr. as the show's villain.

Following the performance, The Menken retired to her suite at the nearby International Hotel, there to wash down oysters with White Star champagne. She fed her traveling companions—her numerous little dogs—sugar cubes dipped in brandy, until drunk, they quit their yapping and fell asleep.[28]

28 In years to come, Adah Isaacs Menken would count as friends and lovers Algernon Swinburne, Henry Wadsworth Longfellow, Walt Whitman, Alexandre Dumas, and Charles Dickens. But then, in a London performance of *Mazeppa!*, her horse bounded out of control, and she was cruelly injured, never to rally. She ceased performing, to die in a backstreet Paris hotel. She was thirty-three years old.

A rare illustration of Adah's ride.

A white man's opium den as illustrated in *Harper's Weekly*.

There were dens not only on the far edge of Chinatown, but along south C Street's "Barbary Coast"— on the route home for hundreds of school kids.

AMUSEMENTS IN Virginia City ranged from a quiet game of checkers or chess to a raucous night on the town, the way lit by the torches of singers, jugglers, and shell gamers. For some, there well might be a visit to the *doves du pave* on down D Street from Maguire's Opera House. And down from Sun Mountain on I Street, on the far side of Chinatown, a nocturnal adventurer might crack the door of "a cave of oblivion":

At first we can see nothing save a small lamp suspended from the center of the ceiling. This lamp burns with a dull red light that illuminates nothing. . . . A voice says: "What do you want?" . . . We feel that we have no business where we are; we simply say, in pigeon-English: "Me comee to see you smokee opium." . . . We now observe that two sides of the den are fitted up with bunks, one above another, like berths on shipboard. A cadaverous opium-smoker is seen in nearly every bunk. These men are in various stages of stupor.

So wrote Dan De Quille. He concluded:

Not a few men—and a few women—are opium smokers. They visit the dens two or three times a week. They say the effect is exhilarating—that it is the same as intoxication produced by drinking liquor except that under the influence of opium a man's brain is almost supernaturally bright and clear. They move no more than dead men. The

V & T trains were renowned as light on the brakes, heavy of the throttle.

eyes of some are wide open, as in a fixed stare. If they have any of those heavenly visions of which we are told, they keep them to themselves, as, save in a few somniloquous mutterings, they utter no sound.[29]

And Mary McNair Matthews was to add:

The opium dens seem to defy all police power to break them up, and are also ruining our people, for many have become slaves to this most destructive habit. Not only men and women visit the opium dens, but I am informed, by good authority, that girls and boys visit them, and often have to be helped home by their companions. It is utter ruin to smoke the first pipe, for there is but one way to keep them from it afterwards, and that way is the walls of an asylum.[30]

ON A FAR BRIGHTER NOTE, come a Saturday morning, Virginia's shops opened at seven, so that holiday-makers could buy new a linen duster or pack a hamper on their way to the Virginia & Truckee station on D Street.

It was a picnic day for Comstockers, an excursion to resorts in the meadows of the Carson Valley.

Like a horse in a starting gate, the day's sturdy little locomotive was anxious to be on its way. It was often the no.11, the Reno, a Baldwin American, puffing smoke and exhaling steam. For engineers and passengers alike, she was the object of considerable affection. Gleaming with brass fittings, "She had sand."

29 *The Big Bonanza*, 295–96.
30 *Ten Years in Nevada*, 259–60.

Reno no. 11. Excursions were offered most every weekend.

Connecting Virginia City with Gold Hill, the first of six tunnels.

The thrill of steaming across Gold Hill's Crown Point trestle, 85 feet high and 500 feet long. And then plummeting down the mountain at a breakneck speed of up to 20 miles an hour.

Crowds of children raced up and down the station's platform. They danced and whirled, the girls with brightly colored ribbons flying from their hair, the boys brushed and scrubbed and by day's end, bound to remedy the situation. Adults were no less excited.

At eight, it was "All Aboard!" and to the clang of the engine's bell, a festive outing was on its way.

Since her beloved husband Sandy's death in 1868 and the failure of their mine, Eilley Orrem had skidded to the edge of poverty. But then, as "The Seeress of Washoe," she had made forays to Virginia City to offer second-sight advice and foretell the future. In her crystal ball, she saw a missing man dead at the bottom of an abandoned shaft, and consoled his loved ones. On a lighter note, she advised Mr. G.L. Whitney as to the whereabouts of his ornate watch chain, and there it was, inadvertently tossed in the rubbish.

Their destination could be either Aaron Treadway's Park or Eilley Orrem's Bowers mansion.

She heard Sam Wagner, the town crier, ringing his bell and offering a $100 reward to anyone who could find a diamond ring lost by a lady on her way home from the Wells Fargo office. She visited the frantic woman, to assured her that the thief who stole it would presently return it. Anonymously, he did.

She'd return to her mansion, its furnishings deteriorating, its once grand gardens, gone to seed.

It was then Sandy to the rescue, materializing in a crystal vision and advising Eilley to make ends meet by making the mansion a resort. "Yes," she told an acquaintance, "Mr. Bowers is always near me, and he directed me to open the mansion for his old friends and their friends and the public generally, and he hopes you will all be much at your ease."

With what remained of a once great fortune, she installed picnic tables and fish ponds, a croquet court and a shooting range. She then hosted the "Champions of the Red Cross," hundreds of same; and the next week there was a "First Grand Annual Rural Entertainment of the Pacific Coast Pioneers." Fifteen flat cars of them, crowded with thousands of picnickers, four brass bands, and untold howling children. The event was a grand, if for Eilley, a tiring success.

The Bowers mansion, now a weekend resort.

Serenading arrivals.

And to come: more excursions! Dancing, singing, children falling into ponds, inebriates loaded in wheelbarrows and trundled to trains departing, thank God, at 4:30 in the afternoon.

The proceeding, understandably, gave otherworldy-inclined Eilley a headache. With some success she'd discourage the crowds—up to four thousand strong—from invading her mansion. That's not to say she wouldn't offer readings and advice to a select few.

In a sitting, Eilley had a vision of a woman leading little children into the night, with banners flying about bearing the names "Sierra Nevada" and "Ophir" (major Constock mines). The woman's clothes fell away, with "her skeleton-like interweaving of veins" symbolizing, Eilley believed, undiscovered silver. But then the woman was knocked down, emblematic of the recent fall of Sierra Nevada stock. Nonetheless, Eilley was confident that "more large ore bodies will be discovered there soon."

———— ·•·‹›·•· ————

There were alternatives to the Bowers mansion or Treadway's Park. In Carson City, one could transfer to Hank Monk's stage and in an hour gain the shore of Lake Tahoe, its waters so transparent that pebbles on its bottom could be distinctly seen at a depth of sixty feet.

Ladies could target shoot, play racquetball, drink, or try their hand at archery.
As well there'd be races for men, boys, and girls. With elaborate prizes for winners.

Eilley's front parlor as a portal
to the beyond.

Her portrait.

Though no one else could see him, Sandy was her comfort.

Aboard a boat on a windless day, one appeared suspended in mid-air. The calm was a tonic, a contrast to the around-the-clock thundering mills of the Comstock.

Whereas no water flowed in Virginia City—excepting the hellish, toxic hot water down in the mines—here it rushed to enhance the majesty of a vast, serene lake.

A wonder of America, the world.

Wrote Dan De Quille (as a mining reporter exploring Virginia's underground hell on a daily basis):

The man of meditative disposition who is weary of the bustle and the strife and the noise and the crowds will wander along by himself and be happy in many a place in the grand solitudes, where whispers from heaven come down through the pines.[31]

Sunday afternoon at the latest, it was time to board a stage or train home. Johnny Waldorf, a child raised and schooled on the Comstock, was to recall, "Because the sun disappeared early, even in summer, picnic trains always returned into blue twilight and a somber, almost mournful world."

31 *The Big Bonanza*, 316.

Lake Tahoe.

Though only thirty-five miles distant, a far cry from Virginia City.

From dinghies to steam yachts, all manner of boats plied Tahoe's waters.

A lakeside cataract.

What little boy didn't enjoy skinning
a branch, baiting a line with leftover lunch,
and fishing for dinner?

R. J. Waters, Photo.   Gold Hill, Nevada.

Pull the wire signaling three bells, then four bells, then three bells, and it was back down to the 1,200-foot level.

Kids

Virginia's first velocipede.

Opposite: Dressed up for a parade: a cigar-chomping Comstock topper and his wife, George Washington on horseback, Lady Liberty, and a scary "Fire Queen and her snakes."

IN WASHOE'S EARLY DAYS, there were no children and just four women: Eilley Orrem, Princess Sarah Winnemucca, and two others. The cry of "Silver!" prompted an influx of ladies of the night, and "The deeper, the richer!" beckoned miners from Croatia to Cornwall to Chile. And with them, their wives and children. Almost overnight, Virginia became a family town. "Finer or more robust children," Dan De Quille ventured, "can be seen in no other town or city in the Union. They grow like mushrooms—and there is nothing to prevent their shooting up and expanding in all directions."

Prosperous for the first time in their lives, miners and their wives sought to give their kids childhoods they never had. They well recalled their danger-fraught days breaking coal in collieries or tending bobbins in textile mills. Here now, an honest miner was paid $3 to $5 a day, which doesn't sound like a lot, but it was, considering that a satisfying dinner at a first-class restaurant cost 60 cents. The Comstock's children were extraordinarily well-dressed. A Boy's Saxony wool fedora went for 25 cents and a dashing Zouave suit for $1; a girl's "extra fine French percale" dress set her parents back 87 cents, plus woven in her hair, gold tinsel braid at 2 cents a yard.[32]

Workers were determined that their children, whether they liked it or not, be lettered and educated, and with the support of a militant Miner's Union, seven schools in Virginia City and four in Gold Hill rose from the dust and sagebrush.

32   In today's dollars, the prices would be 40 to 80 times as much.

Moses. — *Life.* — *Washington.* — *Goddess of Liberty* — *Fire Queen*

sie Coryell — *Lillie Scholl* — *Mark Requa* — *Phoeba Symons* — *Gussie Scott*

Turned-out tots in a goat cart. "Handsomely ornamented with landscape and scroll work," it would have cost a doting father $6.75, more than a going day's wage.

In the four-story Fourth Ward school, a thousand kids slid down bannisters, whistled and shouted, and wouldn't be hushed up. They'd dump pepper on a stove, emptying a classroom. They defied discipline. One of them, young Johnny Waldorf, was to recall, "kids on the Comstock were a contentious lot—cocksure, reckless, bellicose, and without mercy." Experiencing a freedom unknown to their old country or Eastern American forbears, they sassed teachers even if they'd be in for a thrashing. "Scuffling at school" merited

four lashes; "Drinking spirits" was good for eight; "Misbehaving to girls" deserved ten.

Nonetheless, Johnny charitably remembered his first schoolmarm as "a great hearted little woman, who refused to believe that boys were savages."

If not exactly savages, they were daredevils. They'd filch fulminate of mercury blasting caps, good for impromptu fireworks during recess or even in class, in one case frightening a teacher out of her

Hailed as the "finest of its kind on the West Coast, the Fourth Ward school was "Virginia's "Pride and Glory."

Two of Virginia's forty-eight teachers. They'd have their hands full controlling the Comstock's mischief-prone kids.

Sixth grade.

A dime's escape.

wits—at the cost of the thumb and two fingers of a little scholar's left hand.

When a lesson got boring, a geography textbook proved just the right size to conceal a dime novel. There'd be a thrill or two on every page, with a student delighting in the shenanigans of Twilight Charlie or the righteousness of Sheriff Stillwell. Or he'd imagine himself in spunky Jim's boots as he discovered a Big Bonanza. That, after all, was near every Virginian's dream.

Scholars and their good-hearted teachers.

Note the cursive lettering on the blackboard.

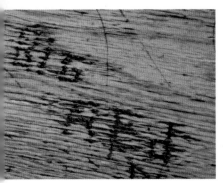 

Big Red and Sophie left their mark.

When the school bell rang at three, teachers would breathe a sigh of relief and gather for coffee and cake before dispersing to second jobs. Making as little as $60 a month, most had little choice but to take in laundry or cut and stitch the fancy frockery popular in Virginia.

At the same time, their schoolgirls, if they had a nickel, would hasten on down C Street to enjoy a phosphate or ice cream in the children's room of the International Hotel and, across the street, admire the fancy goods in the window of Mrs. Meyer's Millinery.

Arriving home, a girl might have helped her mom with housework, curled up with a girl's dime novel, the likes of *The Backwoods Bride* or *The Frontier Angel*—or be scrubbed, combed and fluffed for an excursion to the Sutterley Brothers' photography studio.

As for the boys, they would head for the city's mine dumps, there to scavenge and then sell scrap wood and metal, and if they were lucky, pocket lumps of high grade ore mixed with waste trammed from workings deep beneath their feet. "Life in the dumps never lacked excitement, recalled Johnny Waldorf, "It was a lost day that did not have a fight."[33]

They'd dare each other to tightrope-walk derelict trestles crossing the dumps with, on average, a fall a week. "It seemed as if we were trying to fall the farthest and live." A friend of Johnny's took pride in a sixteen-foot tumble, only to be outdone by a six-year-old boy who'd lost his footing and hurtled down an abandoned mine shaft, his fall cushioned by a pile of dead goats—"but in about ten days the little fellow had fully recovered and was ready for fresh adventures."

The ultimate thrill was to venture into the Comstock's mines, active or forsaken, and Johnny Waldorf was to listen up as he overheard grownups discussing "an old tunnel that in a wandering,

33 This and subsequent quotes are from John Waldorf, *A Kid on the Comstock*, 52–116.

Posing for portraits, some were willing subjects.

Mine dump kids.

Some not.

So much for fancy togs.

Here and there, a scattering of mine dump kids.

drunken way had sought to touch the heart of the mountain." They'd been prospecting it. It had promise.

"Lemme go with you," Johnny asked. "Lemme go with you!" he pleaded. The men yielded, and off into the heart of the mountain they went.

The tunnel forked, then forked again, with one way, Johnny was warned, intersecting the Savage mine's main shaft and a 2,000-foot drop. Up a ladder they went, and on through a maze of levels and drifts.

Arriving at the face they had in mind, the grownups jabbed their candleholders into timbers, and set about drilling. Hammer, quarter turn of a bit, hammer, quarter turn of the bit, hammer . . .

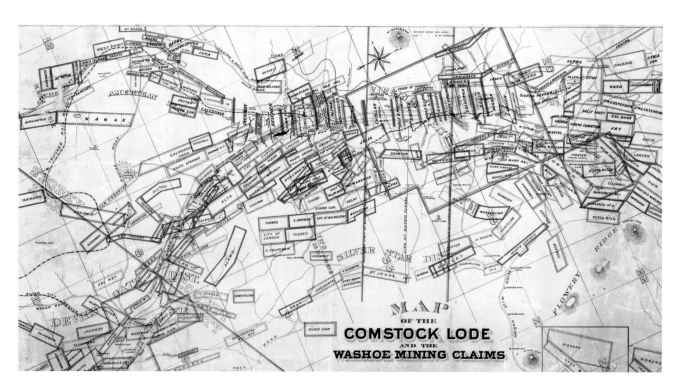

The Comstock as a grand patchwork of claims. The arrow marks a worked-over area where there yet might be silver ore. (A Grafton T. Brown map; he'd created the bird's-eye view of Virginia City on page 26.)

126

One of many abandoned tunnels.

Shifting earth, heavily timbered.

A ladder to a higher level.

128

Past a cave-in.

A miner's sole illumination.

Hammer, quarter turn . . . a mumbled curse . . . hammer, quarter turn.

An hour of this, and Johnny was hungry—and bored. "How long," he asked, with the reply "Two hours more." He fidgeted. One of the grownups asked, "Afraid to go by yourself?" That did it. Borrowing two inches of candle, it was "So long, fellers." And then—

After I got into the tunnel I never looked back, but stooped and hurried on whistling as hard as I could. A whistle wasn't much against a big silence like that but I had to do something. I got along fine for about five minutes, and then my light went out. My heart gave a great thump. My hand went feverishly into my pocket. Not a match! My knees shook.

If I groped on in the dark, I might get into the wrong tunnel and be dashed to death in the Savage shaft. If I stayed where I was and waited for the men to come out, like as not they would have an ore car ahead of them and it would come speeding along the down grade, drowning my cries of alarm and crushing me to death.

I muttered prayers, and stammered as I prayed. I thought of my prized possessions—twenty-seven marbles, including nine crystals and two agates, two tops, a "redhead" baseball, and twenty cents in money. I would have given them all for a match.

Shivering, I went through all my pockets. Then, Joy unimaginable! Stuck deep in a lining, I found half a match. I could hardly hold it to the candle stub. The flame flickered. The flame steadied.

Down a ladder, passing the tunnel to the treacherous Savage shaft, Johnny breathed easier.

Ahead now—light!

The tunnel took a last turn.

It was all easy now. I could see the circle of light. I dropped the candle and never stopped running until God's sun was shining on me!

At last, the light of God's sun.

Kids of the Comstock—and their world.

THAT NIGHT, at the Waldorf's dinner table, Johnny's father might have inquired as to what he'd been up to. "Not much," he may have said, "Learned a bit of geography."

"No dipping a pigtail in an inkwell?"

No answer, but a shake of the head. This was one thing he hadn't done today.

And the conversation may have turned to any number of things. After weathering a slump in the late 1860s, the Comstock's fortunes had revived, but now had slipped, though word was that four Irishmen in their mine down on D Street were onto something. Maybe, maybe not. Or there was the weather. Last week, a wintry Washoe Zephyr had torn up the town, and now clouds were banking over the Sierras. It was cold; it might snow.

If so, Johnny may have brightened, "Can I have a sled?"

SNOW IT WOULD, and Johnny and his friends would be careening down Sutton Avenue and crossing A, B, and C Streets, to where Sutton flattened out on D Street opposite the Con Virginia hoisting works. If only Superintendent Fair's shining carriage was in evidence, they'd trudge back up the hill. Fair had no use for kids, or they for him. But if his partner John Mackay's buggy was there, the boys would be in luck; the good-natured Irishmen would let them tie on their sleds and ride back uptown.

The Comstock's kids looked up to this John Mackay. When there was a performance to their liking, forty or fifty penniless children would gather by the entrance to the Opera House. When Mackay came along, he'd survey the baleful looks, and at the box office ask, "How much for the bunch?"

Johnny Waldorf wrote:

We would enjoy the show, and what is more, we would think better of all mankind. That is why we never envied John Mackay. We wanted him to live forever and always be rich. When he died, we children of the Comstock, though we had not seen him for years, felt that we had lost a near and dear friend.

The Big Bonanza

In 1867, the invention of Giant Powder—dynamite—
expedited a mine's development.

DESTITUTE, THE MINER and the barkeep plodded up the Geiger Grade, an alternate to the route through the Devil's Gate. In sight of Virginia City, the miner—John Mackay by name—rummaged his pockets. Not a dime. "How about you?" he queried his companion, Bill O'Brien.

"Four bits. It's the only money I have in the world."

Mackay picked the coin from O'Brien's palm, and hurled it off into the Nevada sagebrush.

"Whatever did you do that for, John?"

"So we can arrive like gentlemen."

For a time, matters didn't improve. O'Brien polished glasses and doled out whisky. Mackay signed on as a mucker shoveling ore in the Kentuck, a tiny "rat hole" mine all but lost in the Comstock's maze of claims. Even so, he asked to be paid not in cash, but in shares of the faltering company.

If ever there was an "Honest Miner" it was he—humble, hard-working, patient, savvy. And a man of few words; as a child he'd stuttered; as an adult, his speech was slow and deliberate.

In due course, the Kentuck was his—though there wasn't much to the operation; it didn't even have a proper hoist. Matters improved when Mackay purchased a horse, ran a rope over a wheel, and lowered a battered bucket—soon filled with promising ore, promising enough to tidily sell the Kentuck to William Sharon, agent for William C. Ralston's Bank of California. In Virginia City their Bank Ring was relentlessly pursuing a "fortified monopoly"—buying up whatever they could—in the quest to control not only actual mining,

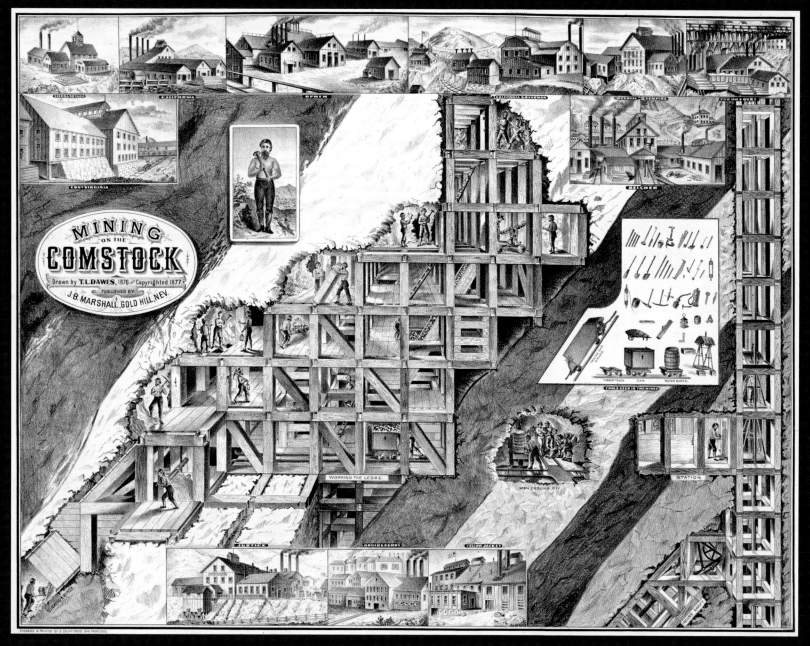

Held open by square set timbers, a stope verges on a bonanza. Look closely, and you can see men cooling off in an ice room. As well, there is an early-day pneumatic drill—fast, efficient, and a "widow maker" as it stirred up clouds of abrasive dust. Or jammed and flew apart.

but everything associated with it, from timber interests to milling operations, all serviced by their Virginia and Truckee Railroad.

John Mackay, emboldened with modest funds, was now to challenge this. And to do so he took on three partners, all Irishmen. In Virginia City, "Slippery Jim" Fair would be on the lookout for properties ripe for acquisition, and once purchased, supervise their operation. William O'Brien would forsake life in a saloon and, along with fellow barkeep James Flood, set themselves up as San Francisco stockbrokers, the better to outfox the Bank Ring on an Exchange trading floor.

The Hale and Norcross Mine was a case in point. Bought with a swift, sly stock trade, it soon turned a handsome profit —and a summons for Mackay to appear at Sharon's Bank of California office.

Mackay would have walked down C Street, and just past the Banner Brothers' clothing store, entered the columned bank to introduce himself to Treasurer W.H. Blauvelt,[34] who with a nod would have directed Mackay's attention to Manager Sharon, emerging from his office to greet Mackay across the rail. If the banker held the miner in disdain, it wasn't apparent, at least at first.

The two men took each other's measure. To Mackay, Sharon was a small, curiously dandified man with a wizened face set with cold gray eyes—that had ruthlessly undone many a mine owner, that had double-crossed well-meaning Adolph Sutro. (It helped to be backed by the clout of San Francisco big money). In a word favored by the *Territorial Enterprise*, William Sharon was Virginia's "Hyena."

34 Of the Arnold & Blauvelt bank, acquired by the Bank of California. (Financial partnerships and associations in Virginia were an inscrutable tangle.)

Close by the site of John Mackay's Kentuck Mine, a still-standing Gold Hill headframe.

The Agency of the Bank of California (to the left).

One of its three massive vaults.

Sharon, on the other hand, may not have been all that aware of Mackay's expertise, despite having lost a bid to acquire the Hale & Norcross. In any case, after a pleasantry or two, he got to the point. As Mackay lacked experience in such things, the ore from his newly prosperous mine should be refined at a Bank of California controlled mill.

Said Mackay, quietly, "I appreciate the offer, Mr. Sharon, but other arrangements have been made."

The ever-calculating Sharon, suddenly, was undone. Flying into a rage, he gestured up C Street to a road out of Virginia. He shouted, "The time is coming when I'll make you pack your blankets back over the Geiger Grade!"

Mackay hesitated, thought about this, considered what was at stake. "W-well, I can do it," he quietly responded, "I packed them in."

And he was out the door.

William Sharon, "the Hyena."

Sharon would have fumed, retreated to his office. Treasurer Blauvelt would have returned to his accounts. Though a Bank of California minion, he was doing quite well for himself, well enough to build a castle on the land he'd purchased up on B Street.

⁃⁃◆⁃⁃

JOHN MACKAY WOULD HAVE enjoyed the fresh air. To him, even mine air, laced with the smoke of Giant Powder, was better than a bank's oppressive smell—stink, really.

C Street would have been abuzz with activity, a "perfect Babel of cries and harangues." A curbside stockbroker cried, "Sure thing if ever there was!" a quack's soap-root toothpowder was touted to "leave the breath pure and sweet, purify the blood, strengthen the nervous system!" And on by the Wells Fargo office, "Only two dollars, gentlemen, takes you to Reno by this splendid Concord coach!"[35] And making his way through a midday throng, John Mackay would have been oblivious to all this, gripped by what he'd said and done. He had drawn a line: on one side, Ralston, Sharon, and twenty-two San Francisco financiers—the *Bank Ring*. On the other, four up-by-their-bootstraps Irishmen.

With the eyes of both camps set on control of the Comstock, this had the makings of a lop-sided face-off. Except that John Mackey had an advantage—as had David in the Good Book. His weapon—his slingshot—would be his unrivaled knowledge of the nature, extent, and prospects of the Comstock lode. He had studied the intricacies of its geology; as a guest of other mine owners, he had descended its shafts and walked its myriad drifts. He understood better than anyone that, though a defined vein ran the length of the city and on under Gold Hill, its highgrade silver occurred in

John Mackay, "the Honest Miner."

35 *The Big Bonanza*, 296–99.

great gobs—bonanzas.[36] Accordingly, from one bonanza to the next, Virginia had reveled in good times—and weathered bad. At present, in the year 1871, times were bad, with all but a few mines in *borrasca*.

From muckers to mine owners, from barflies to preachers, the question was: would there ever be a next big strike? And if so, where?

After John Mackay's confrontation with Sharon, he might well have taken a cross-street down to D Street and, across the way from the Virginia & Truckee train station, walked the surface workings of a cluster of hapless, unproductive mines. He'd examine samples of waste, query miners coming off shift. He had a hunch, a growing glimmer that here, if anywhere, there could be a bonanza. The deepest shaft in the area had reached a 700-foot level, and was on the verge of abandonment. But what about deeper yet—down 1,000 feet or more? Miners put great store in *indications*, fraught with talk of ore shoots and dips, hanging walls and coterminous lenses. In Mackay's reckoning, indications here pointed down, down, down.

Right here, beneath his feet.

Mackay counseled with his partner James Fair, known for his hail-fellow bluster and self-aggrandizement, but sharp when it came to where silver might yet lay hidden. He concurred with Mackay's assessment, and an order was dispatched to San Francisco partners O'Brien and Flood to quietly and quickly acquire a controlling interest of the mines in question. In a critical case they tracked down and courted a stock-rich widow. Just twelve hours later, the Bank of California was on her doorstep. Too late.

The four Irishmen christened their new holding the Consolidated Virginia Mining Company, or easier said, the Con Virginia. They then faced the prospect of sinking a deep shaft—or, as an attractive alternate, arranging to descend another mine's shaft, then tunneling across to their new holdings. But there was a problem with this: the logical shaft was that of the Gould & Curry mine—property of the Bank of California.

In another meeting with Sharon, Mackay held hard feelings in check, took a deep breath, and proposed this. And he couldn't have helped but be stunned when, for an appropriate price, the normally duplicitous, high-handed Sharon agreed. Why? Because in his eyes, Mackay and his Irish friends were the joke of the Comstock.

Sharon would crow to his cashier Blauvelt, "I'll help those Irishmen lose." They were "the forlorn hope of the Comstock."[37]

———————

Partner James Fair supervised the operation. His miners descended the Gould & Curry shaft to its 1,200 level, and commenced tunneling. They had their work cut out for them.

The rock was barren. And a thousand feet later—well inside the Con Virginia's holdings—still barren.

It was dismal work. With minimal ventilation, the air was foul, the heat extreme. Shifts were shortened to fifteen minutes at the face of the tunnel, followed by half hour rests.

But then, Fair noted an almost imperceptible shift in the composition of the rock—and a narrow seam of rich ore, hardly thicker than a knife blade. He ordered his men to follow this, inch by inch. They worked around the clock. They lost the vein, then picked it up again. It widened. At the end of three weeks, it was seven feet

36 Delineated on an 1867 profile. See p. 60.

37 For Sharon there was also the chance that the Irishmen's tunnel would encounter ore while still within the Gould & Curry claim—and they would have no choice but to forfeit their find to the Bank of California.

A foil for erstwhile John Mackay: "Slippery Jim" Fair.

A sample of Con Virginia highgrade.

across, and assaying a respectable $60 a ton. A week later the vein was twelve feet across.[38]

Mackay and Fair were jubilant. They rushed to break ground on a vertical shaft that would tap the newfound ore, ventilate its stifling workings, and hoist its highgrade directly to the surface.

At a depth of 1,167 feet the shaft reached the cap of a silver bonanza like none other on earth, before or since.

And how were the Irishmen characterized? San Francisco rumors circulated that—finding naught—they were simply "getting up a stock deal." Which propelled James Fair to the office of the *Enterprise*, there to shout, "Those city papers have been abusing us long enough! I won't stand it! Where's Dan? Get me Dan! I'll show him what we're doing." And thus summoned, mining reporter Dan De Quille was invited to make a first-hand inspection. Down the shaft and stepping from its cage, De Quille looked up to a roof "shining like a whole casket of black diamonds." Astounded, he was in a chamber 20 feet high and 54 feet wide, with masses of glittering ore everywhere he looked. "The top has been pried off Nature's treasure vault," he declared, and its ore was "going down," no telling how deep.

"For fourteen years," De Quille wrote, "men daily and hourly walked over the ground under which lay the greatest mass of wealth that the world has ever seen in the shape of silver ore, yet nobody suspected its presence."

38 In a contrary opinion, Joseph Goodman, publisher of the *Enterprise*, was to label Fair's account "sheer moonshine." When first encountered, Goodman claimed, the exploratory drift's highgrade silver anything but a sliver in width. "A blind man driving a four-horse team could have followed it in a snowstorm." Further, Fair at the time appears to have been out-of-town, with old-timer Captain Sam Curtis the mine's acting superintendent.

The Con Virginia's seal.

The Con Virginia at the height of its production. Note the timbers soon to go down its shaft and shore up its expanding "Big Bonanza."

#247

Hoisting Men from 3000 ft. Level
of Con. Va. Mine. Virginia City, Nevada.
1875.

At the end of a productive shift.

FLASH LIGHT PHOTO IN 1600 FOOT LEVEL OF C&C

Silver Kings Jim Fair & John Mackay. Underground, they were indistinguishable from $4 a day miners. This photo was long unidentified.

The four Irishmen would be rich beyond imagining. *Silver Kings.* With the largest share, John Mackay would be pronounced "the richest miner on earth." His initial investment, in time, would net him a tidy 35,000 percent profit.

Needless to say, this didn't set well with Ralston, Sharon, and their Bank Ring. Deriding the four Irishmen, they fanned rumors that, like previous bonanzas, theirs was sure to be soon exhausted—and

The late William C. Ralston. His Bank of California
would recover, but never regain its former power.

this notion, shared by others, was to cause a precipitous drop in Con Virginia stock, that had risen from $1.62 a share in 1871 to $710 in 1875, and now fell to $450 a share.

But beware of what you scheme.

The drop in the Irishmen's stock caused Bank Ring holdings to take an even greater dive, to the extent that the mighty William C. Ralston had no choice but to close the Bank of California's San

Francisco doors, and facing personal bankruptcy, wade into San Francisco Bay—and drown. Suicide was suspected, though never proved.[39]

That night, *Hamlet* played in Virginia City, and John Mackay, in his customary box, might well have reflected on the Shakespearian overtones of the drama of his Big Bonanza. He was saddened to hear of Ralston's death, a tragedy. "To die, to sleep. . . . Aye, there's the rub." He had come to admire the banker, in his final year earnest and honest, with Virginia's best interests at heart. But Mackay continued to loathe Ralston's Iago, William Sharon. He was not alone in this. A year ago at an opera house rally, Sharon sought to appease a grumbling audience by admitting, "You know, I can't take my money with me." Whereupon a voice from the gallery called out, "If you did, it would burn!"

39   Thereafter, William Sharon was to take over Ralston's estate, evict his widow from his Belvedere mansion, and move in.

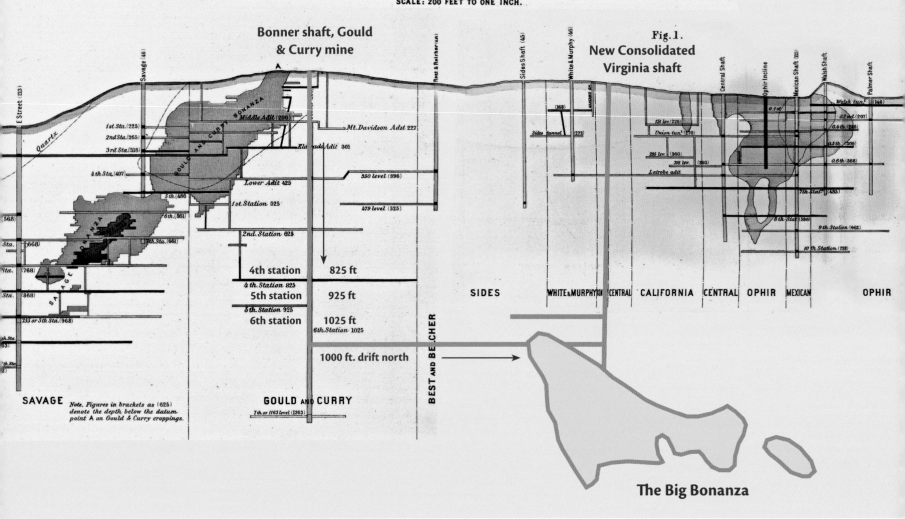

LONGITUDINAL ELEVATION VIRGINIA MINES, COMSTOCK LODE.

SCALE: 200 FEET TO ONE INCH.

Bonner shaft, Gould & Curry mine

Fig. 1.
New Consolidated
Virginia shaft

E Street (213)

Savage (46)

A

Best & Belcher (44)

Sides Shaft (45)

White & Murphy (46)

Central Shaft

Ophir Incline

Mexican Shaft (163)

Walsh Shaft

Palmer Shaft (146)

Quartz

BONANZA

Middle Adit (200)

Mt. Davidson Adit 227

(168)

Walsh tun.¹

1st.Sta.(225)

El dorado Adit 301

Sides tunnel (272)

1st lev. (220)

0.1st

0.2 nd. (207)

2nd Sta.(265)

Union tun.¹ (270)

0.4 th. (240)

3rd Sta.(318)

GOULD AND CURRY

350 level (396)

285 lev. (360)

318 lev. (395)

0.5 th. (309)

4 th. Sta. (407)

Lower Adit 425

Latrobe adit

0.6 th. (368)

(568)

5 th. (486)

1st. Station 525

479 level (525)

7th Stat.¹ (485)

BONANZA

6 th. (561)

8 th. Stat¹ (598)

.Sta. (668)

2nd. Station 625

9th Station (662)

SAVAGE

.Sta. (768)

10 th. Station (738)

.Sta. (868)

4th station   825 ft

735 or 5th Sta. (968)

4 th. Station 825

5th station   925 ft

5 th. Station 925

6th station   1025 ft

6th. Station 1025

SIDES

WHITE & MURPHY
CENTRAL

CALIFORNIA

CENTRAL

OPHIR

MEXICAN

OPHIR

.Sta. 53)

th. Sta. 2)

1000 ft. drift north

BEST AND BELCHER

SAVAGE

*Note. Figures in brackets as (625)
denote the depth below the datum
point A on Gould & Curry croppings.*

GOULD AND CURRY

7 th. or 1163 level (1363)

The Big Bonanza

40th Parallel Survey cross-sections amended to include the Con Virginia's bonanza. The red arrows
mark the risky route to its discovery. A new shaft to the right extracted the bonanza's rich ore.

144

Truth was, rarely in the West would a mine's reality exceed its hype—with the Con Virginia a startling example. And many were the measures of its success: over a million tons of highgrade ore, four staggeringly rich Irishmen, and as James Fair would truthfully boast, "The receipts and expenditures of our Company total more than that of half of the states in the Union."

As the San Francisco *Chronicle* noted,

> Day after day advices from the Big Bonanza show increased value, proving riches before which the treasures of Aladdin's Palace and Monte Cristo's fabulous island pale. . . . This was a bright spot of good honest charity in a desert of fraud and subtle iniquity.

His fire horn in hand, Chief Engineer William Pennison. He was well aware of the threat of major fires.

IN THE HEADY DAYS of the Con Virginia bonanza, there was a glimpse of the future, ignored by most, but heeded by some: a vision of the city's oracle, the "Seeress of Washoe," the widow Eilley Orrem. Gazing her crystal ball, she foretold fire. It was a safe bet. Something or other in Virginia was always going up in flames, cause for six Volunteer Engine and Hook & Ladder Companies, and their proud, brave leather-helmeted and red-shirted volunteers. They called themselves "fire jakeys" and "be Jesus fellows."

Now, Eilley Orrem had not only to gaze her crystal ball, but to look out the window of her Washoe Valley mansion at passing V&T trains laden with mountainsides of Sierra Nevada timber. Their flatcars delivered up to 72,500,000 board feet a year. After the cataclysmic Crown Point disaster,

God forbid another mine fire.

In Carson City's V&T yards, square set timbers en route to Virginia's underground workings.

IN THE EARLY MORNING of Tuesday, October 26, 1875, coming off their graveyard shift, supervisors and miners reported that all was well underground, and braved a Washoe Zephyr as they trudged to their beds for a good day's sleep. As the *Enterprise's* Dan De Quille was to note, "Only the butchers, bakers, and other early risers were astir. The 'owls' of the city, birds of prey that haunt the place all night had disappeared with the gray of dawn."

Excepted was an unnamed drunk who'd picked a fight with his landlady, "Crazy Kate" Shea. In the melee than ensued, a coal-oil lamp was knocked to the floor, and in a moment their boarding house's flimsy walls were aflame.

As to what happened next, Dan De Quille's account, vivid and rueful, is unmatched.[40] At the outset,

When the first fire-bells rang, few persons heeded even though they heard them. Soon, however, the mournful and long-drawn wail of one steam whistle after another, in quick succession, was heard to join in sounding the alarm till the fierce clangor of the bells was almost drowned. The bells, loudly as they rang, only said: "There is a fire," but in the fierce, wild shriek of the whistles there was that which thrilled all and which said as though with a human voice: "There is a fire, and a great and most dangerous one!"

Persons of all ages and every condition were fleeing for their lives in all stages of dress and all manner of undress. Many had only time to leap from their beds and rush into the streets, as their houses were wrapped in fire.

Adding to the fear of fire, there'd been a number of disturbing omens—disturbing not only by Eilley, but by a population stoked with the superstitions of countries from China to Slovakia. In late 1874 Virginia City was wracked by a furious, blinding snowstorm. Yet clamber up Sun Mountain, and all was calm and clear, and there was a stunning eclipse of the moon. A few weeks later, a column of flame shot heavenward over by the Ophir mine. But there was no smoke. Rather, the men who dared approach were awestruck by "a weird whiteness" resembling "a shooting spire of the aurora borealis." Then, as suddenly as it appeared, the eruption was gone, vanished down an abandoned mineshaft.

Omens, fate, fire. In the parlor of her Washoe Valley mansion, Eilley Orrem feared for the charmed city up the hill. She predicted its destruction, and in its wake a great snow storm.

40 A last chapter in his *The Big Bonanza*, 428–436.

To be expected in a tinderbox town.

Rung to no avail.

Indeed, the whole air seemed on fire; the whole face of the mountain a sea of fire.

To thwart the holocaust, fire companies dynamited building after building in its path. Nevertheless,

> The flames soon reached the International Hotel, the principal hotel of the city and a huge brick structure, and it became a volcano of fire. About the same time, farther to the southward, the Bank of California, the *Enterprise* building, and many large brick and stone structures from three to five stories in height were vomiting fire from every window and door from roof to basement. Churches were towering pillars of fire.

At the Con Virginia, John Mackay and James Fair ordered the mine's shafts covered with a makeshift heavy wooden platform,

to be heaped with dirt and sand. If the fire reached the masses of timbers of their bonanza, it could well spread to the whole of the mines of the northern Comstock, and with the "breath of hell," doom Virginia City.

In the midst of this, an old woman was said to have approached Mackay, telling him that St. Mary of the Mountains church, to the west of his mine, was on fire. He reportedly replied, "Damn the church, we can build another if we keep the fire from going down these shafts!" A conflicting account has Mackay ordering St. Mary's dynamited, then promising Father Manogue he'd build a grander church in its place. Whatever the case, St. Mary's was destroyed, and the fire raged north to the surface workings of the Con Virginia, there to consume a million feet of stored timber, and penetrate its hastily sealed shafts.

With tenacity and at considerable risk, firemen followed the fire underground, and furiously working hand pumpers fed by stretched hoses, saved the day.

As reported in the next issue of the *Enterprise* (printed in neighboring Gold Hill),

> About eleven o'clock on Tuesday, out of the crater of the conflagration there emerged a man haggard with fatigue, begrimed with dust, powder-smoke, and the smoke of the fire. He looked like a laborer just ready to drop from exhaustion. It was John Mackay.

Come three in the afternoon, a final firestorm down C Street left Virginia City "a universal wreck." As John Mackay headed home, he joined "people wandering through the debris with such a look on their faces as men and women wear when they gather round a coffin." A pall of smoke and mercury fumes had everyone coughing

The International Hotel—and every other structure in this image—was burned to the ground.

The Con Virginia's extensive surface workings. Drawn in 1875, the year of their destruction.

A last image of St. Mary's in the Mountains (no. 7).

The edge of destruction.

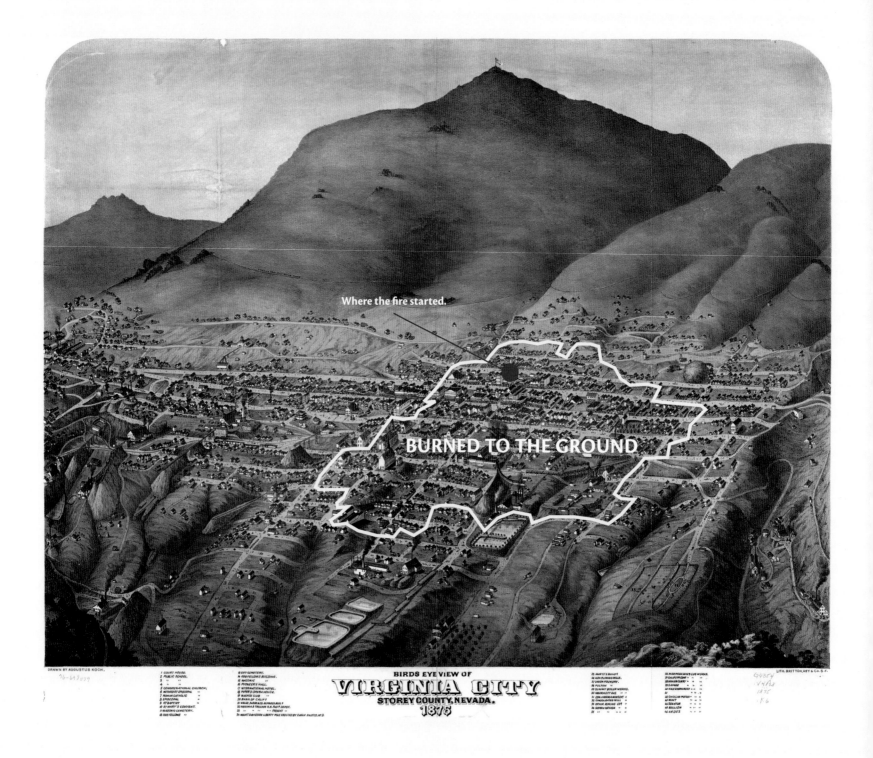

Where the fire started.

BURNED TO THE GROUND

As it remains: Blauvelt's mansion.

As it once was: Mackay's bungalow.

and spitting, but thankfully, the V & T was offering free passes down the hill. Nearly every major businesses and 500 homes had been destroyed—including Mackay's modest bungalow. Ironically, a few hundred feet away a castle rose in untouched, ostentatious splendor—the residence of W.H. Blauvelt, William Sharon's Treasurer at the Bank of California.

That night, the Washoe Zephyr that had fanned the flames toppled what remained of once imposing buildings. Come midnight, it started to snow, shrouding a blackened wasteland in a mantle of glistening white.

Would Virginia ever recover, regain its devil-may-care repute? For an answer, consider an ore car. These stout little hoppers had a capacity of 1,600 to 1,800 pounds, and (with Con Virginia ore assaying at up to $633 of silver a ton), a full load would be worth about $540. Multiply this by some 400 carloads a day, then translate this sum to contemporary dollars, and the take would be in

the neighborhood of $7,000,000—each and every day. *And from a single mine.*

What better reason for Virginia, as mythology's phoenix, to rise from its ashes?

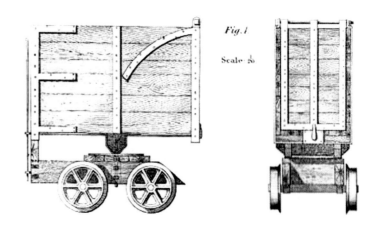

The INTERNATIONAL HOTEL

Leaving the Carson City yards—to the rescue.

AS FIRE SWEPT THE CITY, the engines and rolling stock of the V & T were hustled down the hill, out of harm's way to the railroad's Carson City yards. And now, as snow in Virginia City gave way to mud, they came roaring back. The workhorse Genoa no. 12, the favorite Inyo no. 11, and eighteen others—returned with up to forty-five runs around the clock laden with food, clothing, tents, and timber. The little short line, though conceived in Bank Ring greed, was to become the city's lifeline, a harbinger of hope.

A wave of what-the-hell optimism swept Virginia. Even as ashes were hot and sparks still sputtered, people were hammering up frame buildings. Swaying walls were toppled; new foundations laid.

A priority was the rebuilding and reopening of the Con Virginia mine. John Mackay set a sixty-day deadline for this—and with a week to spare, hundreds rejoiced as the mine's hoisting engine whirred into action, and miners dropped 120 stories into the heart of the glittering Big Bonanza.

The Con Virginia, on schedule, declared a handsome dividend.

By night, on up the hill from the Con Virginia, the city glowed in the light of hundreds of gas lamps hoisted aloft, so that reconstruction could be rushed around the clock.

In a matter of months, not years, Virginia was its old self. As Dan De Quille wrote, "The gap left in the city was again filled, and was not readily distinguished by strangers, except by its striking resemblance to new patches on an old pair of pantaloons."

A prominent patch on those old pantaloons was a new, iconic International Hotel, symbol of everything the city was—and could be. A reporter for *Frank Leslie's Illustrated*

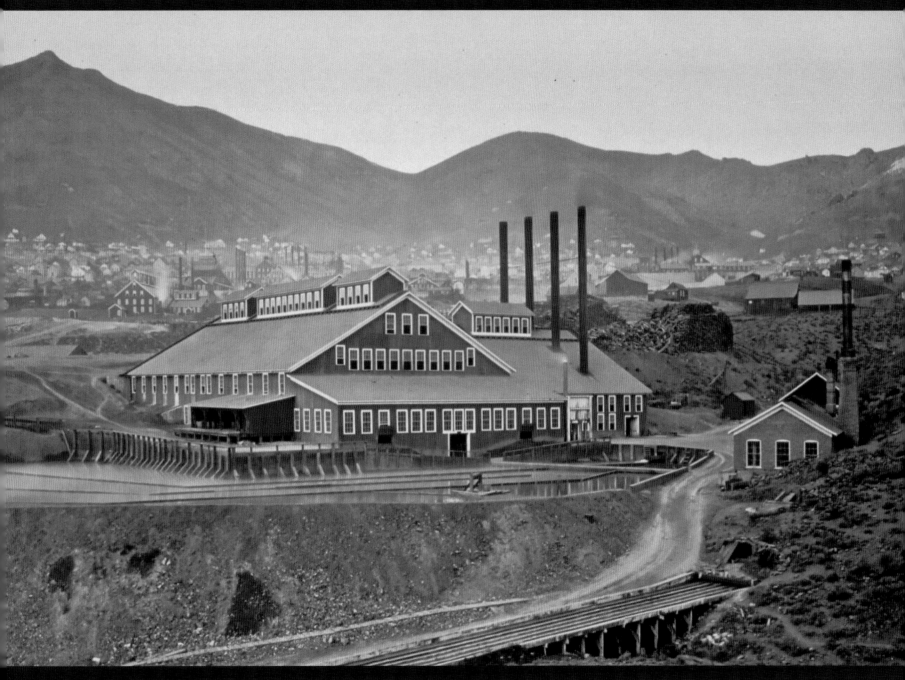

The Con Virginia's new pan mill—"put up in better style than before the fire."

With rare exception, Virginia City's buildings date to 1875 and later—after the great fire.

Looking north on C Street — to, on the left, a third edition of Virginia's International Hotel.

Newspaper found it to be "a new and handsome brick building . . . so fresh and spotless in its white paint, so immaculate in all its appointments, from the flaming red velvet and snowy lace curtains of the parlor to the least accessory of the large dining-room."

The cuisine was said to rival that of New York, or even Paris. Caviar, truffles, oysters galore, and lobsters shipped on ice from the waters of the Atlantic.

Gents were offered darkly paneled reading and smoking rooms, and for "the best in libations," a place at the brass rail of Pidge and Patterson's resplendent International Saloon. Ladies refreshed themselves in a fashionable retiring room, there to rest on velvet sofas beneath crystal chandeliers. And not to be overlooked, in their special room children perched on soda fountain stools.

With 144 luxe rooms, the International was proclaimed the finest hostelry between Salt Lake and San Francisco.

The hotel drew guests from across the world, and was the setting for dances where ladies wore gowns imported from Gagelin's and Worth's[41] of Paris, and admired the effect in mirrors of French plate framed with hand-carved laurel scrolls. As the *Enterprise* observed,

41 The wellspring of haute couture.

A celebratory crowd thronging the pride of the richest place on earth.

◀ Who exactly they were is unknown—but they spared nothing in their dress. ▶

Matilda Heron.

J. W. Smith

The impression the congregated company gave to modest outsider was that no people had better clothes than Virginia people; that no one knew better how to put on their clothes or, or to wear them worthily. It was just a blaze of glory.

"The people here seem to run to jewelry," added a correspondent for the *New York Tribune*, "and the number of diamonds displayed quite overwhelms one's senses. I have never been in a place where money is so plentiful, nor where it is spent with so much extravagance and recklessness."

A local observer shook her head at the sight of "ladies dresses so rich and gaudy, in silks and satins, wearing a whole flower garden on the top of their heads."[42]

And favored horses were shod with silver shoes.

⸻✦⸻

As a classic grand hotel, the International hosted famed guests, paramount among them the staggeringly rich—if uncomfortably so—John Mackay. As long as he remained in Virginia City, he would be a resident. At the end of a day at his mine, he'd either spend some time with old friends in the back room of Dr. Cole's drug store, or stop by the swank Washoe Club, where he would lament to Dan De Quille that since no amount he could conceivably win at cards could excite him, life hardly seemed worth living. Be that as it may, at 9 p.m. sharp, he would enter the International's back B Street door, and passing up its "rising room" (elevator in those days), climb the five flights of stairs to his top floor suite 5, where attended by a single Chinese servant, he'd read, combat his stutter before a mirror, and leading the life of a quiet bachelor, turn

42 *Ten Years in Nevada*, 131–32.

in for the night. His wife, Marie Louise, a Virginia City seamstress when he courted her, had decamped to the social swirl over in the city by the sea, San Francisco, and thence to Paris.

Mackay would regularly rise at 4 a.m. to pull on a miner's boots and garb, and soon, with a candle lantern in hand, prowl and inspect his Big Bonanza. Was the ore blasted free on the previous shift still highgrade? Was there an end of it all in sight? No, not yet. This was his world, his passion—the risks and chances of mining.

For Mackay, there was reverie in this, his candlelit world. The smell of Giant Powder, footsteps echoing down drifts, the argot of Honest Miners, and at the heart of it all, a great, glittering chamber. By comparison, the ballrooms of mighty mansions were naught.

John Mackay. Comfortable in a battered hat, a miner's coarsely woven smock and worn denim trousers.

Aboveground, Mackay was a different man altogether.

On returning to the International, Mackay would on occasion be buttonholed for advice, for which he had a stock answer. As he told Dan De Quille, "I say to all that come to me: 'Go put your money in a savings bank." He chuckled, then continued, 'You should see some of them stare at me when they hear this advice. They evidently consider me a strange kind of mining man. But in speaking so I mean just what I say, and my advice is good. I never advise people to buy mining stocks of any kind.'"

He was indeed "a strange kind of mining man." Quiet and straightforward on the surface, he'd at times fight to control a fiery rage. He appeared the ultimate Honest Miner, yet he was willing to have O'Brien and Flood engineer lucrative stock deals on his behalf, and he tolerated Jim Fair's slippery ethics in amassing their joint fortunes.

———————————

A FREQUENT INTERNATIONAL GUEST, Adolph Sutro, had finally at last completed his tunnel. From beginning to end, it had been a tough go. Nearing the Comstock, the heat was "sufficient to cook a chicken in half an hour," and ventilation at the header was all but nonexistent. This was hard on the miners, and harder on their mules who, despite being watered and rubbed with ice, were overcome with spasms, and injured workman as they fell over dead, "as if shot."

Finally, the night came when a miner withdrew his drill, and a rush of hot air whooshed through the drill hole. And then, from the other side, a miner was to ask, "Has Sutro ordered the champagne?"

Though Sutro and Mackay would have inevitably crossed paths in the public rooms of their hotel, their relationship was, at best, frosty. Mackay believed the tunnel too little, too late. And in many ways it was, which Sutro himself realized. He would sell out—but not just yet.

————◆————

ACTORS AND ACTRESSES at Piper's Opera House across the way (a rebuilt successor to Maguire's), frequented the International. And there was the matter of the mysterious Mrs. George Allen. A grand hotel needs a mystery woman, and she fit the bill. Although she dressed in black, she was not in deep mourning. Rather, she sparkled with diamonds. The object of considerable gossip, she was dubbed "the $990,000 diamond widow." And tongues wagged all the more when she entered the hotel's dining room on the arm of ever-natty Adolph Sutro. They quaffed champagne; they savored quail on toast.

Then came the evening when the hotel's elegant calm was rent by a woman screaming for help. With guests at his heels, the International's proprietor rushed to source of the cries, burst into a suite, and beheld Leah Sutro—*Mrs. Adolph Sutro*, in from San Francisco—battering Mrs. George Allen with a champagne bottle. Too bad for the "diamond widow"; worse for Adolph. He pleaded innocence. No matter, his marriage was ruined.

————◆————

AS THE YEAR 1878 drew to a close, the Comstock gloried in a run of six bonanza years, in which close to three million tons of ore had been milled, and valued at $365,939,129. In today's dollars: a sum somewhere between $10 billion and $15 billion. Yet there was a growing unease, borne of the simple and inescapable logic that the more the silver that came out of the ground, the less remained. But as in the past, there'd be a next bonanza. Wouldn't there? The theory

Adolph Sutro.

Find the top-hatted man resting his head on his hand, and consider the pump's size.

was that, as a "true fissure vein" welling up from deep, deep in the earth, the only obstacle to the Comstock's future success would be a lack of wherewithal to probe its depths.

Now abuilding, there was a monument of sorts—a mighty contraption—to put any such qualms to rest.

It was a pump, the likes of which had never been seen before or since. Built at the behest of John Mackay, it could clear the way for mining 4,000 or more feet beneath the city.

Visitors tarrying at the International Hotel were invited to behold the Union shaft's Cornish pump, and pronounced it "a wonder." It had a forty-foot flywheel weighing 110 tons. A 300-ton pump rod plunged down a 2,500-foot shaft. The mighty machine would hoist two million gallons of water every twenty-four hours.

Hope for a next, deeper bonanza.

Such was Virginia's fame that this 1878 image was printed in Germany. Note the finery and the calm (a contrast to a rough-and-ready similar view sixteen years earlier, page 21).

of Union and some other of the steep cross streets," and a brave few may have attempted the two-and-a-half mile plunge to Devil's Gate. In the same issue, the paper described that, despite the storm:

> A regular raid was made on the stores where fancy article and toys were on sale. All the stores, indeed, were crowded with customers. Everybody was buying something. Whatever losses may have been sustained, let them be forgotten during the holiday season.

On December 24, the celebratory "sound of the trumpet, drum, harp, tom-tom, zim-zim and whoola-whoola are heard in the land." They accompanied appearances of Old Zern, Little Holly, and Sunelta, Queen of the Frost Fairies.

"Tons and tons of turkeys have been sold." And many were donated to the poor, earning benefactors "white marks in the Big Book."

That night, there was a pageant at the Fourth Ward School, carols and services at a host of churches, and milk and cookies set out for Santa.

On Christmas day, the International Hotel set a grand table. A menu survives. Its wine list features a choice of eight champagnes and is garnished with the likes of *Foies de Dinde Saute, Sur Croustead aux Champignons*—an far cry from a miner's beef, beans, and bread, (the "three Bs") of Virginia's pioneering days.

The dinner conversation would have inevitably turned—as it long had—to the city's fortunes. Optimism prevailed. Wasn't that what the Union pump was all about? Yet there were disquieting signs. Some months back, faced with empty rooms, the International had

---

COME CHRISTMASTIDE of 1878, calm, civility, and a cheery joy were abroad in Virginia's streets. Rivals and combatants of old—the likes of Sharon and Mackay—amiably chatted in the International's public rooms.

The city's wooly years were history.

ON DECEMBER 20, Christmas trees rumbled into town in V&T ore cars, to be decorated up and down C Street, and according to the *Territorial Enterprise*, "were set up in the churches and private dwellings. What wonders the little folks will find upon the branches of these trees in due season."

Three days later, it snowed, and that night the newspaper reported that "coasting was lively among the boys on the upper part

162

cut its rate to $2.50 a night, and encouraged regulars to become permanent residents at $55 a month, meals included. Assays were off; brokers were subdued in their "sure thing" offerings. In a town long rife with rumors, few—if any—were noised of new strikes. The *Enterprise* was to lament,

> We shall have our usual doses and sorrows to-morrow in the shape of the San Francisco stock reports. How they will sit on stomachs leaded with roast turkey remains to be seen.

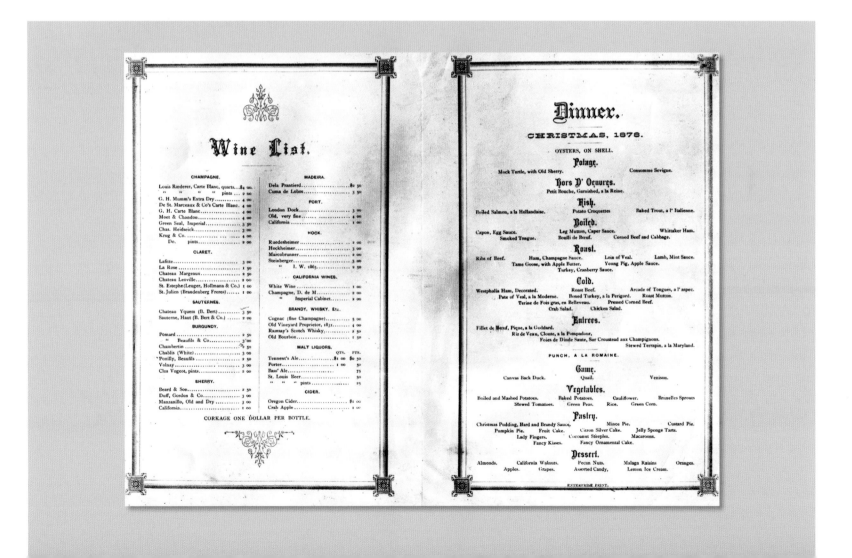

The Lake Tahoe steamer *Meteor*.

But, begone dull care!

That night there were rival celebrations: a "National Guard Social with music by Barney's Quadrille Band," and a Bachelor Club's "Grand Bon-Bon Social," promised to be "a real jolly, chatty, good, old-fashioned affair."

———————

IN OCTOBER of the following year, crowds lined the shore of Lake Tahoe anxious for a glimpse of a man on a round-the-world tour, and up in Virginia, the International Hotel's reception and accolade would be hard to match.

The steamer *Meteor* hove into view. The crowd cheered; a brass band struck up the National Anthem.

The party—including the man's wife, son, and daughter-in-law—disembarked and a few hours later, arriving in the V & T's palace car "California," they was greeted by fifteen hundred school children and near every last citizen of Gold Hill and Virginia City.

A six-horse carriage whisked the man through "triumphal arches and gay hangings" to the International, where the register was signed:

Finished at last.

America's former president was in for a heady three nights and two days, beginning with a state dinner and ending with his review, from the hotel's balcony, of a parade featuring Civil War veterans, every last fire company, and a contingent of Paiutes decked out in war paint.

A highlight of the visit would be an underground tour. Ulysses S. Grant was keen to see, first hand, the source of the hundreds of millions in silver bullion that had maintained the value of the American dollar in the course of reconstruction following the Civil War.

Explosions of Giant Powder welcomed Grant to the mouth of the Sutro tunnel, where "much merriment was occasioned by the general's appearance in the costume of a miner." The party boarded mine cars, and for thirty-five minutes—thirty-five very long minutes—rode to the heart of the Comstock. It was an otherworldly experience, scary even, as their mules clopped on through miasmic heat and eternal night. To keep up their spirits, the party sang "The Stars Spangled Banner" and "The Sweet By and By." (Good for a man who once said he knew only two tunes: " 'The Battle Hymn of the Republic' was one; the other wasn't.")

Extricating himself from the cramped mine car and continuing on foot, the general witnessed a demonstration of the bone-shaking pneumatic drills new to the Comstock. All the better to extract the ore; hard on the ears.

The humidity hung in underground clouds. Water dripped, ran in muddy rivulets between the party's boots.

And the heat. The general had never experienced such heat. He gamely trudged on, and listened to explanations offered by one or the other of his hosts. He nodded, forced a smile. His ears rang.

There was "a sense of horrible confinement."

A hard-pressed mule. Some, born underground, never saw the light of day.

Finally, on the rattling ride to the surface, there was the matter of trusting the skill and judgment of a single hoist operator. God forbid that he'd whet his whistle on his way to work.

The way was flanked by miners. How on earth could they survive this, day-in, day-out?

Up the shaft, out of the cage, the party gathered for a photograph. Left to right: John Mackay, Mrs. M.G. Gillette, U.S. Grant, Jr., Mrs. Grant, General U.S. Grant, S. Yanda, Mrs. E.G. Fair, Governor J.A. Kinkead, James Fair.

IN THE PHOTOGRAPH of the Grant party, two people are notably missing people. One would be Adolph Sutro. The scandal of his alleged dalliance with the mysterious Mrs. Allen preyed upon his sense of Victorian morality, and he thought it best if he didn't accompany the ex-President.

The other would be John Mackay's wife, Marie Louise. It's not that she hadn't been down the Virginia Con's shaft. She had, and at the 1,500-foot level was taken with its treasure chamber gleaming with silver crystals. "Can I have enough," she reportedly asked John, "enough silver from our own mine to make a memorable thing? A dinner service, I think." With a shrug and a smile, Mackay agreed, and thereupon shipped half a ton of refined silver to New York's Tiffany & Co., where 200 craftsmen would spend two years completing 1,250 individual pieces—the largest, the grandest, the most ornate dinner setting of its time.

Marie Louise Mackay.

The general was queried: did he enjoy his two hour tour? He blurted, "That's as close to hell as I ever want to get!"

In the meantime, Marie Louise had embarked on an arc of social conquest. Leaving John to foot the bills in Virginia City, she had tired of San Francisco, was snubbed in New York, and in a grand Pompeian-themed mansion, took up residence in Paris.

With the Con Virginia reliably under control, John paid annual visits, and made little effort to conceal his disdain for his wife's circle of Parisian friends. He was a man of few words, and in this case they were "bums and parasites." When the Tiffany silver arrived and was served up at banquets, he'd make a point of using the wrong fork or spoon (with nineteen choices of the latter). When a fading aristocrat trumpeted his heritage, he'd counter with stories of his Irish "bogtrotter family" and their living room shared with a cow and pigs. When he'd had enough, he would send a coded message to

PANORAMA DES PALAIS

Panorama des Palais.

his San Francisco money man, who on cue would dispatch a cable summoning him back to America on urgent business.

None the wiser, Marie Louise gloried in her role in the upcoming 1878 Paris Exposition.

The occasion featured the sculpted head and shoulders of the Statue of Liberty, a gift from the people of France to the people of America. As well, there was a gift from Mr. to Mrs. Mackay: her over-the-top silver service. On one hand, it was a taste of the great wealth of the Comstock Lode; on another, it garnered backhanded whispers of *tres gauche* and like derision.

Louis Comfort Tiffany himself was at a loss as to what to call the collection. Persian perhaps? Or Mogul? He settled on *Indian.*

Whatever it was, a correspondent for the New York *Daily Tribune* weighted in: "The service is a monument of the wealth of the owner." All told, it was "an accumulation of coin and cunning." Certainly on Marie Louise's part; perhaps on John's as well.

Bound for New York.

A forty-eight pound, solid silver punch bowl.

Amidst the clutter, three-foot candelabras.

A caddy for gents' cigars.

The view east from A Street.

BACK IN THE NEVADA DESERT, up in Virginia City, above and below ground, there was a pervasive, growing gloom, a realization that an end was in sight.

At the International Hotel, notable guest Sutro checked out, never to return. He'd quietly unloaded his stock in his tunnel and was off to San Francisco, where he'd be elected the city's mayor.

In his later years.

Over the next few years, one by one, the Comstock's great mines were in *borrasca*, and ceased operations. Their hoists and pumps were freighted to newer, promising camps. Or sold for scrap.

In 1880 the Con Virginia declared a last dividend. Its Big Bonanza was exhausted.

The International Hotel dropped its permanent guest rate to $12.50 a month.

In 1884 the Union shaft's great Cornish pump—with only a whisper of ore to its credit—was shut down.

John Mackay had held out hope that a new bonanza would be found at greater depth, but now, that hope had proved a humbug. All that remained of the Comstock Lode, he acknowledged, was "a poor man's pudding."

In 1886 Mackay ordered the Con Virginia's pumps shut down. The mine flooded. Con Virginia stock bottomed out at 5 cents a share.

In these, the city's twilight years, John Mackay could nevertheless look back on all he had done for Virginia and all that the place and its people meant to him. From a vantage point near his early bungalow home (now a vacant lot) the imposing International Hotel (his last home here) rose to the left, and to the right there was the spire of St. Mary's of the Mountains. In the wake of the great fire of 1875, he had quietly underwritten the church's reconstruction.

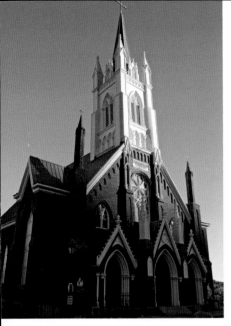

If ever the city deserved a requiem, this would be the place, an isle of serenity in a whistle-shrieking, dynamite-blasting, stamp-thundering world.

Epilogue

Dame Fortune

Approaching Virginia City.

Though the population had dwindled from more than 25,000 to less than 2,700, the spirit of the place was intact. In winter's cold, teeth might chatter, but spirits were resolute, no matter that stock in the Ophir mine—Virginia's first great bonanza—sold for a penny a share, down from a high of $1,400. As a latter-day business directory noted, "When 'stocks are down' it will be observed that Virginians do not hang their heads like devotees of Dame Fortune in other towns less elevated. The atmosphere will not admit of it. Humor and pleasant sociability prevail."

Clearing the track for passengers and freight.

In this painting by John Gast, Dame Fortune promises Western adventurers a glorious destiny. In Virginia City, for many, she delivered just that. But now, in the words of 1800s mining historian Charles Shinn, "The goddess, so long wooing these stumbling men, tires at last and turns away with laughter in her eyes. Thither the Goddess looks, choosing new favorites. Already those whose day is done are forgotten."

By the first decade of the next century, near all of Virginia's great enterprises had failed—save one, the Virginia & Truckee Railroad, the pride of a community that was damned if it would become a ghost town.

A derailment taken in stride.

The *Territorial Enterprise*—"the grand old rag"—survived until May of 1916.

C Street deliveries, with a glimpse of the
International Hotel in the background,
before it once again burned to the ground
in December of 1914.

A sampling of souls drawn to the Comstock . . .

Schnitzer's Nevada Brewery—for an ever-thirsty, if dwindling populace.

A stove to stoke; a ledger to keep.

A Brunswick mine shift boss and his crew.

Visiting French actresses venture underground, to exclaim, "Zee heat is indescriptible!"

Comstockers and visitors about to witness what
all the excitement was about. They're all gone now,
many at rest in Virginia's Silver Terrace cemeteries.

The Silver Terrace had sections dedicated to Masons,
West Coast Pioneers, Knights of Pythias, Roman Catholics,
Redmen, Firemen, and Oddfellows.

Killed in 2,000-foot-
level accident.

Depressed. Took her life with strychnine.

A corner of the Masons' section, with tombstones carved by Hugh Muckle. With "scarcely a day that there is not one or two funerals among the miners," he rarely lacked business.

Overdosed on morphine.

Died in a stagecoach accident.

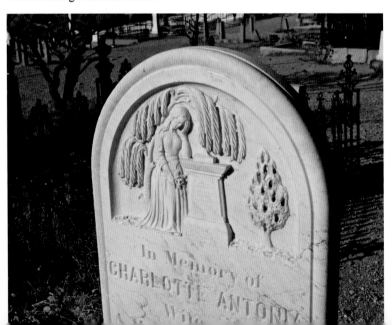

Death, no one will dispute, is joyless. But that said, Virginia's Silver Terrace graves testify to lives lived in one of the most extraordinary places on earth, an isolated mountain town that danced with the devil in its headlong rush for riches. And in so doing, its populace sampled a goodly number of the seven deadly sins, notably avarice. Yet this was tempered by virtues: hard work, for one—and humor, the latter exemplified and egged on by the likes of C. Ross Browne, Dan De Quille, and Mark Twain.

Further, there was the sense that folks weren't simply going about their business, but as actors on a sagebrush stage, they were players in an ongoing, suspense-packed drama, be their role comedic, tragic, heroic, or smacking of villainy. Rare was the soul that here led a dull life, or that regretted life on the hill.

All the world's a stage…

They gloried in pranks, pints, and grand flush times. They loved Shakespeare, and for good reason: they had their own King Henry, Iago, and in abundance, Falstaffs. Indeed, at Maguire's and Piper's Opera Houses, Virginians could startle a touring Prospero by, in ragged chorus, joining him in the recital of:

You do look, my son, in a moved sort,
As if you were dismayed. Be cheerful, sir.
Our revels now are ended. These our actors,
As I foretold you, were all spirits, and
Are melted into air, into thin air.

For souls at rest in the Silver Terraces,

We are such stuff
As dreams are made of, and our little life
Is rounded with a sleep.

The Gold Hill depot.

Once welcoming forty-five trains a day.

Not forgotten: the V & T.

The Crown Point mine's gallows frames.

ACKNOWLEDGMENTS

The author is indebted to the lives and stories—by turns gripping and touching—of Virginians in their glory days. Walk C Street an hour before dawn, and you rub shoulders with their ghosts, be they reeling from saloons or trudging to a morning shift in the steaming depths in the earth.

Their triumphs, their shenanigans, their spirit in the face of adversity—all were epic.

I thank the welcoming, knowledgeable staffs of the city's C Street Visitor Center, the Comstock History Center, and the Fourth Ward School. And I appreciate the access to remnants of the city's vast underground workings preserved by the Chollar Mine and the Ponderosa Saloon (with its drift to the Best & Belcher Mine).

Considering that hundreds upon hundreds of photographs were destroyed in Virginia City's great fire of 1875, locating surviving images was a challenge, with a particular thanks to Lee Brumbaugh of the Nevada Historical Society in Reno, Sue Ann Monteleone at the Nevada State Museum in Carson City, Lara Mather at Virginia's Fourth Ward School, Susan Snyder at Berkeley's Bancroft Library, and Jeff Bridger at the Library of Congress.

It was a pleasure working with the enthusiastic and understanding folks at Sunbelt Publications. Publications manager Debi Young kept the project running smoothly down the rails, copy editor Anita Palmer righted grammatical wrongs, designer Lydia D'moch captured the spirit and gusto of the era, and editors Diana and Lowell Lindsay were ever encouraging, insightful, and good company.

Finally, a heartfelt thanks to my wife Bonnie. Every step of the way, she was along on a journey that had us imagining and reliving what it would have been like to rattle up a 1200-foot shaft, blink in the sunlight, clean up, dress in our starched best, have a restorative nip at a two-bit saloon, and cheer The Menken as she rode to the rafters of Maguire's Opera House.

PHOTOGRAPHY CREDITS

The book's droll woodcuts and etchings are by J. Ross Browne for his *A Peep at Washoe* (1860) *and Washoe Revisted* (1865); True Williams and Roswell Shurtleff for Mark Twain's *Roughing It* (1872); and the anonymous illustrator of Dan De Quille's *The Big Bonanza* (1876).

Multiple photographs on a page are listed clockwise from upper left (a-b-c-d). If known, photographers and artists are credited in boldface.

Not listed below: color photographs taken by the author.

Cover:	Bird's-eye lithograph, **Augustus Koch**
	Insert: Nevada Historical Society
i	Historic Fourth Ward School Museum
ii–iii	Library of Congress, **Carleton Watkins**
v	National Geographic Society, **Winfield Parks**
vi–vii	Huntington Library
ix	Nevada Historical Society
x a	Author's collection
x b	Huntington Library
xi b	Society of California Pioneers, **Lawrence & Houseworth**
xii a	Author's collection
xii b–xiii	Sandy Pavel
xvi	Author's collection
xvii	Library of Congress
6–7	Nevada Historical Society
9–10	Western Nevada Historic Photo Collection
11 a	Huntington Library

The Virginia City Photography Club.

11 b	Author's collection
26–28 a	Library of Congress, **Grafton T. Brown**
28 b	Nevada Historical Society
31	Library of Congress, **Augustus Koch**
32–33 b	Nevada Historical Society
34 a	Lucius Beebe
35	Library of Congress, **Augustus Koch**
36	Nevada Historical Society
37	Nevada Historical Society, **Sutterley Brothers**
41	Bancroft Library, University of California, Berkeley
43 a	Author's collection
43 b	Nevada Historical Society
46	National Portrait Gallery

103	California Historical Society	152	Western Nevada Historic Photo Collection
104	Houghton Library, Harvard Theater Collection	153	Bancroft Library, University of California, Berkeley
105–106	Author's collection	155	Special Collections, University of Nevada, Reno
107	Western Nevada Historic Photo Collection	156 b	Nevada Historical Society
108 a–b	Nevada State Museum	156 d–e	Special Collections, University of Nevada, Reno
109	Special Collections, University of Nevada, Reno	157–158	Nevada Historical Society
110 a	Nevada Historical Society	159	Special Collections, University of San Francisco
110 b	Historic Fourth Ward School Museum	160 a	Nevada State Museum
111	Special Collections, University of Nevada, Reno	160 b	Huntington Library
113–116 a	Society of California Pioneers, **Lawrence & Houseworth**	161	Special Collections, University of Nevada, Reno
116 b	Special Collections, University of Nevada, Reno	162 a–b	Author's collection
117	Historic Fourth Ward School Museum	163 a–b	Nevada Historical Society
118–119	Nevada Historical Society	164 a	Special Collections, University of Nevada, Reno
120	Nevada State Museum	164 b	Author's collection
124 b	Historic Fourth Ward School Museum	165	Nevada State Museum
123–124 a	Historic Fourth Ward School Museum	166a	Nevada Historical Society
125 a	Author's collection, **Sutterley Brothers**	166 b	Society of California Pioneers, **Lawrence & Houseworth**
125 b	Huntington Library	167 a	Nevada Historical Society
125 c	Nevada Historical Society	166–167	Special Collections, University of Nevada, Reno
125 d	Author's collection, **Sutterley Brothers**	168–170 b	Special Collections, University of Nevada, Reno
126 a	Library of Congress	170 a–b	Author's collection
126 b	Author's collection	172 a	Nevada Historical Society
132	Nevada Historical Society	172 b	Special Collections, University of Nevada, Reno
135	Author's collection	174 a	Bancroft Library, University of California, Berkeley
137 a	Bancroft Library, University of California, Berkeley	174 b	Nevada State Museum
138 a	Library of Congress, **Matthew Brady**	175	Autry National Center
138 b	Nevada Historical Society	176	Special Collections, University of Nevada, Reno
140 a	Library of Congress	177–178 a	Nevada Historical Society
141	Bancroft Library, University of California, Berkeley, **Carleton Watkins**	178 b	Author's collection
		179 a	Nevada Historical Society
142–143a	Nevada Historical Society	179 b–180	Huntington Library
143 b	Bancroft Library, University of California, Berkeley	181	Nevada Historical Society
144	Library of Congress	182–183	Historic Fourth Ward School Museum
145 a	Nevada Historical Society	187	Mark Hammon
145 b	Nevada State Museum, **Carleton Watkins**		
147	Special Collections, University of Nevada, Reno		
149–150	Library of Congress, **Augustus Koch**		
151 b	Nevada Historical Society		
151 c	Author's collection		

SELECTED BIBLIOGRAPHY

The book's 1800s sources are a delight—lively, informative, often slyly humorous.

1860	J. Ross Browne, *A Peep at Washoe; or, Sketch of Adventure in Virginia City* (reprinted by Lewis Osborne, Palo Alto, 1968)
1861–1916	Issues of the *Territorial Enterprise* (master microfilms available at The University of Nevada, Reno and Las Vegas: the Nevada Historical Society, Reno; and the Nevada State Library, Carson City)
1865	J. Ross Browne, *Washoe Revisited* (reprinted by Biobooks, Oakland, n.d.)
1872	Mark Twain, *Roughing It* (with an excellent edition offered by Oxford University Press, New York & Oxford, 1996)
1873	*The Virginia and Truckee Railroad Directory, 1873-74, Embracing a General Directory of Residents of Virginia City, Gold Hill, Silver City . . .* (available as a Nabu Public Domain reprint, 2012)
1876	Dan De Quille, *The Big Bonanza: an Authentic Account of the Discovery, History, and Working of the World-Renowned Comstock Lode of Nevada* (reprinted by Alfred A. Knopf, New York, 1947)
1883	Eliot Lord, *Comstock Mining and Miners* (reprinted by Howell-North, Berkeley, 1959)
1896	Charles Howard Shinn, *The Story of the Mine* (reprinted by the University of Nevada Press, Reno, 1980)

More recently, there are:

Grant H. Smith, *The History of the Comstock Lode 1850-1920* (Nevada Bureau of Mines and Geology, 1943)

Lucius Beebe & Charles Clegg, *Legends of the Comstock Lode* (Stanford University Press, Stanford, 1950)

John Taylor Waldorf, *A Kid on the Comstock: Reminiscences of a Virginia City Childhood* (American West Publishing Company, 1970)

Warren Hinkle & Fredric Hobbs, *The Richest Place on Earth: the Story of Virginia City and the Heyday of the Comstock Lode* (Houghton Mifflin, Boston, 1978)

Douglas McDonald, *Virginia City and the Silver Region of the Comstock* (Nevada Publications, Las Vegas, 1982)

Ronald M. James, *The Roar and the Silence: a History of Virginia City and the Comstock Lode* (University of Nevada Press, Reno, 1998)

Michael J. Makley, *John Mackay: Silver King in the Gilded Age* (University of Nevada Press, Reno, 2009)

Keith F. Davis & Jane Aspinwall, *Timothy H. O'Sullivan: the King Survey Photographs* (Nelson Atkins Museum of Art, Kansas City, Missouri, 2011)

Richard F. Lingenfelter, *Bonanzas & Borrascas: Gold Lust and Silver Sharks* (Arthur H. Clark Company, Norman, Oklahoma, 2012).

Readers interested in additional sources and background may contact the author via Sunbelt Publications, PO Box 191126, San Diego, CA 92119–1126.

INDEX